Contents

Introduction	4
General	5
Bedfordshire	6
Cambridgeshire	15
Cheshire	29
Cumberland	40
Derbyshire	40
Durham	43
Essex	46
Hertfordshire	47
Huntingdonshire	49
Lancashire	54
Leicestershire	56
Lincolnshire	58
Northumberland	60
Nottinghamshire	67
Rutland	67
Staffordshire	70
Suffolk	70
Warwickshire	72
Westmorland	75
Yorkshire	75

Introduction

War memorials are of interest to a wide range of people. Family historians may be able to identify their ancestors from them; local historians use them to trace local participation in war; they could provide useful information to enable military buffs to fill in the history of particular regiments. There is also interest in them as works of art.

This interest is demonstrated by the extraordinary number of web sites devoted to war memorials, which it is the purpose of this book to list. The prime aim has been to identify web pages which provide names, and which relate to a particular locality. Sites which are merely photographic, without names, are excluded, as are sites dealing with overseas memorials.

Some rolls of honour are also included, but these have not been systematically searched for. Nor has there been any attempt to systematically search for regimental sites.

This book lists web pages rather than web sites, since some sites include numerous pages relating to many different places. The titles of each page are given as they appear on the page; where no title is given, I have indicated this by enclosing my own title in square brackets. I have added annotations where necessary, usually to indicate the conflict(s) memorialised.

Arrangement is by county and place, with some general sites listed in the first chapter, and, where necessary, at the beginning of each county chapter.

If you are unable to find a URL listed here, you should enter either a part of the URL itself, or words from the title, into a search engine such as www.google.com.

It is inevitable that there will be errors in a book of this kind. If you spot any, please let me know. It is also a fact that URLs change frequently, and no doubt a small proportion of those listed here will be out of date within a few months of publication. Again, please let me know if you come across such changes.

It is hoped to produce new editions of this listing at frequent intervals, in order to help you keep track of the information currently available on the web.

This book has been typed by Cynthia Hanson, and seen through the press by Bob Boyd. My thanks to them, and also to the officers of the Federation of Family History Societies, whose support is vital to my work. My wife Marjorie is also to be thanked for insisting that I turn the computer off occasionally!

Stuart A. Raymond

War Memorials on the Web

PART 2
The Midlands, Northern England and East Anglia

Stuart A. Raymond

FEDERATION OF FAMILY HISTORY SOCIETIES (PUBLICATIONS) LIMITED

Published by
The Federation of Family History Societies (Publications) Ltd.
Units 15-16, Chesham Industrial Estate
Oram Street, Bury
Lancashire BL9 6EN

in association with:
S.A. & M.J. Raymond
P.O.Box 35
Exeter EX1 3YZ
Email: samjraymond@btopenworld.com
Webpage: www.samjraymond.btinternet.co.uk/igb.htm

ISBNs:
ation of Family History Societies: 1-86006-171-0
S.A. & M.J. Raymond: 1-899668-31-4

First published 2003

Printed and bound by The Alden Group, Osney Mead, Oxford OX2 0EF

General

Introductory Sites

- Do you Remember? English and Welsh Roots and Remembrance Day
  globalgazette.net/gazfd/gazfd42.htm
  Article

- Sacrifice Remembered. Memorials of the Great War and the Language of Remembrance
  www.sassoonery.demon.co.uk/warmems.htm

- United Kingdom War Memorials
  www.hellfire-corner.demon.co.uk/memorials.htm
  General discussion

- War Memorials: Remembered in Stone
  www.aftermathww1.com/memoria.asp
  General discussion

Institutions

- Commonwealth War Graves Commission
  www.cwgc.org/

- Imperial War Museum: Rolls of Honour
  www.iwm.org.uk/lambeth/famhist2.htm
  Brief note on its collection

- UK National Inventory of War Memorials
  www.iwm.org.uk/collections/niwm/index.htm

- Friends of War Memorials
  www.marple-uk.com/misc/fowm.htm
  Society home-page

- DTI's War Memorials
  www.dti.gov.uk/warmemorial/index.htm
  Memorials to staff of the Department of Trade and Industry

- Officers Died
  redcoat.future.easyspace.com/
  Lists of names from various campaigns, 18-20th c.

Web Page Collections

- Great War Churches
  www.btinternet.com/~james.fanning/greatwar/index.html

- Ray Westlake's War Memorial Corner
  www.hellfire-corner.demon.co.uk/memcorner.htm
  Collection from Herefordshire, Worcestershire and the Welsh Borders, *etc.*

- War Memorial Name Transcripts
  med441.bham.ac.uk/Warmems/index.html

Boer War

- A Survey of Memorials to the Second Anglo-Boer War in the United Kingdom and Eire
  www.bowlerhat.com.au/sawvl/essay04.html

- Anglo-Boer War Memorials Project
  members.aol.com/abwmp/briefing.htm

- Boer War Memorials
  med441.bham.ac.uk/WarMems/boerindex.html

World War I

- Soldiers Died in the Great War: soldiers and officers died in the First World War 1914-19
  www.great-war-casualties.com/index2.htm
  Details of a CD

- H.M.S. Hood Rolls of Honour: Memorials to Hood's lost
  hmshood.com/crew/memorial/memorial.html
  Covers 1916-41.

World War II

- Army Roll of Honour: World War II: Soldiers Died in the Second World War 1939-45
  www.world-war-2-casualties.com/
  Details of a CD

- Battle of Britain Roll of Honour
  www.raf.mod.uk/bob1940/roll.html

- 44th Royal Tank Regiment 1939-1945 Roll of Honour
  uk.geocities.com/williamfdungey/mems/44roll.html

- Fleet Air Arm Archive 1939-1945: Roll of Honour and Personnel Register
  www.fleetairarmarchive.net/RollofHonour/Index.html

Falkland Islands
- Falkland Islands History Roll of Honour
  www.raf.mod.uk/falklands/roll.html

Gulf War
- Roll of Honour: In Honour of the British Sailors, Soldiers and Airmen who gave their lives for the liberation of Kuwait, August 1990-July 1991
  www.britains-smallwars.com/gulf/Roll.html

Links
- British Memorials
  www.simonides.org/links/memorials/memorials-uk.html
  Links to sites, mainly overseas memorials or of general interest

- United Kingdom War Memorials
  www.ww1photos.com/LinksWarMemorials.html
  Links to local war memorial sites

- Soldiers Memorials
  www.angelfire.com/mp/memorials/memindz1.htm
  Many pages of overseas memorials to British soldiers

Bedfordshire

General
See also Cambridgeshire
- Bedfordshire War Memorials & Rolls of Honour
  www.roll-of-honour.com/Bedfordshire/index.html

- Bedfordshire & Hertfordshire Regimental Memorial
  www.roll-of-honour.com/Bedfordshire/KempstonWarMemorialBarracks.html
  World War II and other 20th c. conflicts.

- Bedfordshire Police Roll of Honour
  www.roll-of-honour.com/Bedfordshire/BedfordshirePoliceRollofHonour.html
  World War I

- Bedford: Bedfordshire Boer War Memorial
  www.roll-of-honour/Bedfordshire/BedfordBoerWarMemorial.html

- Bedfordshire Regiment: Memorial in Christchurch, Rawalpindi
  www.angelfire.com/mp/memorials/bedsmem.htm
  1891-4

Ampthill
- Ampthill Roll of Honour
  www.roll-of-honour.com/Bedfordshire/AmpthillStAndrewsRollofHonour.html
  World Wars I & II

Arlesey
- Arlesey Roll of Honour
  www.roll-of-honour.com/Bedfordshire/ArleseyRollofHonour.html
  World Wars I & II

Aspley Guise
- Aspley Guise Roll of Honour
  www.roll-of-honour.com/Bedfordshire/AspleyGuiseRollofHonour.html
  World Wars I & II

Barton
- Barton: War Memorial
  www.roll-of-honour.com/Bedfordshire/BartonRollofHonour.html
  World Wars I & II

Battlesden

- Battlesden War Memorial
  www.roll-of-honour.com/Bedfordshire/BattlesdenRollofHonour.html
  World War I

Bedford

- Bedford Modern School: Memorials
  www.roll-of-honour.com/Bedfordshire/BedfordModernSchoolMemorials.html
  Boer War and World War I

- Bedford St. Leonards Roll of Honour
  www.roll-of-honour.com/Bedfordshire/BedfordStLeonardsRollofHonour.html
  World War I

- Bedford, St. Paul's C of E: Rolls of Honour
  www.roll-of-honour.com/Bedfordshire/BedfordStPaulsRollofHonour.html
  For the North-West Frontier, the Boer War, World War I,the West
  Indies 1866-9, *etc.*

- Bedford St. Paul's Methodist: Roll of Honour
  www.roll-of-honour.com/Bedfordshire/
  BedfordStPaulsMethodistRollofHonour.html
  World Wars I & II

- Bromham Road Methodist, Bedford: Roll of Honour
  www.roll-of-honour.com/Bedfordshire/
  BedfordBromhamRoadRollofHonour.html
  World Wars I & II

Biddenham

- Biddenham Roll of Honour
  www.roll-of-honour.com/Bedfordshire/BiddenhamRollofHonour.html
  World Wars I & II

Biggleswade

- Biggleswade War Memorial
  www.roll-of-honour.com/Bedfordshire/BiggleswadeRollofHonour.html
  World Wars I & II, and Malaya

Bletsoe

- Bletsoe: Roll of Honour
  www.roll-of-honour.com/Bedfordshire/BletsoeRollofHonour.html
  World Wars I & II

Blunham

- Blunham: Rolls of Honour
  www.roll-of-honour.com/Bedfordshire/BlunhamRollofHonour.html
  World Wars I & II

Bolnhurst

- Bolnhurst. St. Dunstan's Church: War Memorial
  www.roll-of-honour.com/Bedfordshire/BolnhurstRollofHonour.html
  World War I

Bromham

- Bromham St. Owen: Roll of Honour
  www.roll-of-honour.com/Bedfordshire/BromhamStOwenRollofHonour.html
  World War I & II

Campton

- Campton: Rolls of Honour
  www.roll-of-honour.com/Bedfordshire/
  CamptonRecreationGroundRollofHonour.html
  World Wars I & II

Cardington

- Cardington Roll of Honour
  www.roll-of-honour.com/Bedfordshire/CardingtonRollofHonour.html
  World Wars I & II

- Cardington R101 Memorial
  www.roll-of-honour.com/Bedfordshire/CardingtonR101.html
  Airship disaster, 1930

Carlton

- Carlton St. Mary: Roll of Honour
  www.roll-of-honour.com/Bedfordshire/CarltonStMaryRollofHonour.html
  World Wars I & II

Chalgrave

- Chalgrave (Tebworth) Memorial Hall: Roll of Honour
  www.roll-of-honour.com/Bedfordshire/ChalgraveRollofHonour.html
  World Wars I & II

Clapham

- Clapham War Memorial
  www.roll-of-honour.com/Bedfordshire/ClaphamRollofHonour.html
  World Wars I & II

Clifton
- Clifton Village Roll of Honour
  www.roll-of-honour.com/Bedfordshire/CliftonRollofHonour.html
  World Wars I & II

Clophill
- Clophill War Memorial
  www.roll-of-honour.com/Bedfordshire/ClophillRollofHonour.html
  World Wars I & II

Cockayne Hatley
- Cockayne Hatley: Roll of Honour
  www.roll-of-honour.com/Bedfordshire/CockayneHatley.html
  World War II

Cople
- Cople Roll of Honour
  www.roll-of-honour.com/Bedfordshire/CopleRollofHonour.html
  World Wars I & II

Cotton End
- Cotton End Village Memorial
  www.roll-of-honour.com/Bedfordshire/CottonEnd.html
  World Wars I & II

Cranfield
- Cranfield Roll of Honour
  www.roll-of-honour.com/Bedfordshire/CranfieldRollofHonour.html
  World Wars I & II

Dunstable
- Dunstable Roll of Honour
  www.roll-of-honour.com/Bedfordshire/DunstableRollofHonour.html
  World Wars I & II

Dunstable Downs
- Dunstable Downs, Robertson Corner: Roll of Honour
  www.roll-of-honour.com/Bedfordshire/DunstableDownsRobertsonCorner.html
  World War I

Dunton
- Dunton War Memorial
  www.roll-of-honour.com/Bedfordshire/DuntonRollofHonour.html
  World War I

Eaton Bray
- Eaton Bray
  www.users.waitrose.com/%7Ehinchie/Villages/Eaton__Bray/EatonBray.htm
  War Memorials, World War I & II

- Eaton Bray Roll of Honour
  www.roll-of-honour.com/Bedfordshire/EatonBrayRollofHonour.html
  World Wars I & II

- Eaton Bray Wesleyan: Roll of Honour
  www.roll-of-honour.com/bedfordshire/EatonBrayWesleyanRollofHonour.html
  World War I

Eaton Socon
- Eaton Socon Roll of Honour
  www.roll-of-honour.com/Bedford/EatonSoconRollofHonour.html
  World Wars I & II

- Eaton Socon (Beds): Roll of Honour
  www.roll-of-honour.com/Huntingdonshire/EatonSocon.html
  World Wars I & II

- Eaton Socon War Memorial
  www.huntscycles.co.uk/Memorials/Eaton%20Socon.htm
  World wars I & II

Eggington
- Eggington: Roll of Honour
  www.roll-of-honour.com/Bedfordshire/EggingtonRollofHonour.html
  World Wars I & II

- Eggington
  www.users.waitrose.com/%7Ehinchie/Villages/Eggington/Eggington.htm

Elstow
- Elstow War Memorial
  www.roll-of-honour.com/Bedfordshire/ElstowVillageRollofHonour.html
  World Wars I & II   Elstow 19th Century War Memorials

  www.roll-of-honour.com/Bedfordshire/Elstow19thCenturyRollofHonour.html
  World Wars I & II

- Elstow F.E.P.O.W. Memorial
  www.roll-of-honour.com/Bedfordshire/ElstowFEPOWMemorial.html
  Far East prisoners of war, World War II

- Elstow, Bedford County School: War Memorial
  www.roll-of-honour.com/Bedfordshire/
      ElstowBedfordCountySchoolRollofHonour.html
  World War I

- Elstow Bunyan Meeting: Roll of Honour
  www.roll-of-honour.com/Bedfordshire/
      ElstowBunyanMeetingRollofHonour.html
  World War I

Eversholt

- Eversholt: War Memorial
  www.roll-of-honour.com/Bedfordshire/EversholtRollofHonour.html
  World Wars I & II

Everton

- Everton: Roll of Honour
  www.roll-of-honour.com/Bedfordshire/EvertonRollofHonour.html
  World Wars I & II, *etc.*

Eyeworth

- Eyeworth Roll of Honour
  www.roll-of-honour.com/Bedfordshire/EyeworthRollofHonur.html
  World War I

Felmersham

- Felmersham & Radwell Memorials
  www.roll-of-honour.com/Bedfordshire/FelmershamRollofHonour.html
  World Wars I & II

Flitton

- Flitton & Greenfield War Memoriald
  www.roll-of-honour.com/Bedfordshire/GreenfieldRollofHonour.html
  World Wars I & II

Flitwick

- Flitwick Roll of Honour
  www.roll-of-honour.com/Bedfordshire/FlitwickRollofHonour.html
  World Wars I & II

Goldington

- Goldington Roll of Honour
  www.roll-of-honour.com/Bedfordshire/GoldingtonRollofHonour.html
  World Wars I & II

Great Barford

- Great Barford Village Hall & Church: Rolls of Honour
  www.roll-of-honour.com/Bedfordshire/
      GreatBarfordVillageHallRollofHonour.html
  World Wars I & II

Greenfield

See Flitton

Harlington

- Harlington War Memorial
  www.roll-of-honour.com/Bedfordshire/HarlingtonRollofHonour.html
  World Wars I & II

Harrold

- Harrold: Roll of Honour
  www.roll-of-honour.com/Bedfordshire/HarroldRollofHonour.html
  World Wars I & II

Haynes

- Haynes Roll of Honour
  www.roll-of-honour.com/Bedfordshire/HaynesRollofHonour.html
  World Wars I & II

Heath & Reach

- Heath and Reach War Memorial
  www.users.waitrose.com/%7Ehinchie/Heath/heath_%2B_reach.htm

- Heath and Reach: Roll of Honour
  www.roll-of-honour.com/Bedfordshire/HeathandReachRollofHonour.html
  World Wars I & II

Henlow

- Henlow War Memorial
  www.roll-of-honour.com/Bedfordshire/HenlowRollofHonour.html
  World Wars I & II

- Henlow St. Mary Churchyard: War Memorial
  www.roll-of-honour.com/Bedfordshire/HenlowStMaryRollofHonour.html
  World War II

- R.A.F. Henlow St. Andrew: Roll of Honour
  www.role-of-honour.com/Bedfordshire/HenlowStAndrewChurchRAF.html
  20th c. memorials

Higham Gobion

- Higham Gobion: War Memorial
  www.roll-of-honour.com/Bedfordshire/HighamGobionRollofHonour.html
  World War I

Houghton Conquest

- Houghton Conquest War Memorial
  www.roll-of-honour.com/Bedfordshire/HoughtonConquestRollofHonour.html
  World Wars I & II, and the Korean War

Houghton Regis

- Houghton Regis Parish Church: Roll of Honour
  www.roll-of-honour.com/Bedfordshire/HoughtonRegisChurchRollofHonour.html
  World Wars I & II

Hulcote

- Hulcote & Salford Roll of Honour
  www.roll-of-honour.com/Bedfordshire/SalfordRollofHonour.html
  World Wars I & II

Husbourne Crawley

- Husbourne Crawley: Roll of Honour
  www.roll-of-honour.com/Bedfordshire/HusbourneCrawleyRollofHonour.html
  World Wars I & II

Ickwell Green

- Ickwell Green (Northill Parish) Memorial
  www.roll-of-honour.com/Bedfordshire/IckwellGreenRollofHonour.html
  World Wars I & II

Kempston

- Kempston Cemetery: War Graves
  www.roll-of-honour.com/Bedfordshire/KempstonCemetery.html
  World Wars I & II, and later conflicts

- Kempston: Roll of Honour
  www.roll-of-honour.com/Bedfordshire/KempstonRollofHonour.html
  World Wars I & II, and the Korean War

Keysoe

- Keysoe War Memorial
  www.roll-of-honour.com/Bedfordshire/KeysoeRollofHonour.html
  World War I

Knotting

- Knotting Roll of Honour
  www.roll-of-honour.com/Bedfordshire/KnottingRollofHonour.html
  World War I

Langford

- Langford War Memorial
  www.roll-of-honour.com/Bedfordshire/LangfordRollofHonour.html
  World Wars I & II

Leagrave

- Leagrave War Memorials
  www.roll-of-honour.com/Bedfordshire/LeagraveRollofHonour.html
  World Wars I & II

Leighton Buzzard

- Leighton Buzzard
  www.users.waitrose.com/%7Ehinchie/leightonbuzzard/leighton__buzzard.htm
  War Memorial

- Leighton Buzzard: Roll of Honour
  www.roll-of-honour.com/Bedfordshire/LeightonBuzzardRollofHonour.html
  World Wars I & II

- Leighton Buzzard Beaudesert School: Roll of Honour
  www.roll-of-honour.com/Bedfordshire/
  LeightonBuzzardBeaudesertRollofHonour.html
  World Wars I & II, and Korean War

- Leighton Buzzard Cedars School
  www.roll-of-honour.com/Bedfordshire/LeightonBuzzardCedarsRollofHonour.html
  World War II

- Leighton Buzzard Commercials: Rolls of Honour
  www.rolls-of-honour.com/LeightonBuzzardCommercialRollofHonour.html
  Memorials at the bank and the Post Office, World Wars I & II

- Leighton Buzzard: Salvation Army: Rolls of Honour
  www.roll-of-honour.com/Bedfordshire/LeightonBuzzardSARollofHonour.html
  World War I

Little Staughton
- Little Staughton: Roll of Honour
  www.rootsweb.com/engbdf/LittleStaughtonRollofHonour.html
  World Wars I & II

- Little Staughton R.A.F. Book of Remembrance, no. 109 & no. 582
  Squadrons
  www.roll-ofhonour.com/Bedfordshire/LittleStaughtonBookofRemembrance.html
  World War II

Lower Gravenhurst
- Lower Gravenhurst: War Memorial
  www.roll-of-honour.com/Bedfordshire/LowerGravenhurstRollofHonour.html
  World Wars I & II

Luton
- George Kent Ltd., Luton: Roll of Honour
  www.roll-of-honour.com/Bedfordshire/LutonGeorgeKentLtdRollofHonour.html
  World War I

- J. W. Green Ltd., Luton: War Memorial
  www.roll-of-honour.com/Bedfordshire/JWGreenRollofHonour.html
  World War I

Marston Moretaine
- Marston Moreteyne: Roll of Honour
  www.roll-of-honour.com/Bedfordshire/MarstonMoreteyneRollofHonour.html
  World Wars I & II

Maulden
- Maulden Village War Memorial
  www.roll-of-honour/Bedfordshire/MauldenRollofHonour.html
  World Wars I & II

Melchbourne
- Melchbourne Roll of Honour
  www.roll-of-honour.com/Bedfordshire/MelchbourneRollofHonour.html
  World Wars I & II

Meppershall
- Meppershall War Memorial
  www.roll-of-honour.com/Bedfordshire/MeppershallRollofHonour.html
  World War I

- Meppershall. St. Mary's Church War Memorial
  www.roll-of-honour.com/Bedfordshire/MeppershallStMaryRollofHonour.html
  World War II

Millbrook
- Millbrook Roll of Honour
  www.roll-of-honour.com/Bedfordshire/MillbrookRollofHonour.com
  World Wars I & II

Milton Ernest
- Milton Ernest: Roll of Honour
  www.roll-of-honour.com/Bedfordshire/MiltonErnestRollofHonour.html
  World Wars I & II

Moggerhanger
- Moggerhanger: Roll of Honour
  www.roll-of-honour.com/Bedfordshire/MoggerhangerRollofHonour.html
  World Wars I & II

Northill
See Ickwell Green

Oakley
- Oakley Roll of Honour
  www.roll-of-honour.com/Bedfordshire/OakleyRollofHonour.html
  World Wars I & II

Odell
- Odell All Saints. Roll of Honour
  www.roll-of-honour.com/Bedfordshire/OdellRollofHonour.html
  World Wars I & II

Old Warden

- Old Warden War Memorials
  www.roll-of-honour.com/Bedfordshire/OldWardenRollofHonour.html
  World Wars I & II

- Old Warden Village Memorial
  www.roll-of-honour.com/Bedfordshire/OldWardenRollofHonour-5.html
  World Wars I & II; several pages

Pavenham

- Pavenham: Roll of Honour
  www.roll-of-honour.com/Bedfordshire/PavenhamRollofHonour.html
  World War I

Pertenhall

- Pertenhall. St. Peter's Church: War Memorial
  www.roll-of-honour.com/Bedfordshire/PertenhallRollofHonour.html
  World War I

Peters Green

- Peters Green / Perry Green: Roll of Honour
  www.roll-of-honour.com/Bedfordshire/PetersGreenRollofHonour.html
  World War I

Podington

- Podington Roll of Honour
  www.roll-of-honour.com/Bedfordshire/PodingtonRollofHonour.html
  World War I

Potton

- Potton Roll of Honour
  www.roll-of-honour.com/Bedfordshire/PottonRollofHonour.html
  World Wars I & II

Pulloxhill

- Pulloxhill: Village War Memorial
  www.roll-of-honour.com/Bedfordshire/PulloxhillRollofHonour.html
  World Wars I & II

Radwell

See Felmersham

Ravensden

- Ravensden: Roll of Honour
  www.roll-of-honour.com/Bedfordshire/RavensdenRollofHonour.html
  World Wars I & II, and Lucknow, 1881

Renhold

- Renhold Roll of Honour
  www.roll-of-honour.com/Bedfordshire/RenholdRollofHonour.html
  World Wars I & II, and the Battle of Alma, 1854

Ridgmont

- Ridgmont Roll of Honour
  www.roll-of-honour.com/Bedfordshire/RidgmontRollofHonour.html
  World War I & II

Riseley

- Riseley War Memorial
  www.roll-of-honour.com/Bedfordshire/RiseleyRollofHonour.html
  World Wars I & II

Roxton

- Roxton: Roll of Honour
  www.roll-of-honour.com/Bedfordshire/Memorials/RoxtonRollofHonour.html
  World Wars I & II

Salford

See Hulcote

Sandy

- Sandy War Memorial
  www.roll-of-honour.com/Bedfordshire/SandyRollofHonour.html
  World Wars I & II

Sharnbrook

- Sharnbrook: Roll of Honour
  www.roll-of-honour.com/Bedfordshire/SharnbrookRollofHonour.html
  World Wars I & II

Shefford

- Shefford Roll of Honour
  www.roll-of-honour.com/Bedfordshire/SheffordRollofHonour.html
  World Wars I & II

Shillington

- Shillington Village War Memorial
  www.roll-of-honour.com/Bedfordshire/ShillingtonVillageRollofHonour.html
  World Wars I & II

- Shillington Chapel War Memorial
  www.roll-of-honour.com/Bedfordshire/ShillingtonChapelRollofHonour.html
  World War I

Silsoe

- Silsoe War Memorial
  www.roll-of-honour.com/Bedfordshire/SilsoeRollofHonour.html
  World Wars I & II

Slip End

- Slip End / Woodside, Luton: War Memorial
  www.roll-of-honour.com/Bedfordshire/SlipEndWoodsideRollofHonour.html
  World Wars I & II

Souldrop

- Souldrop Roll of Honour
  www.roll-of-honour.com/Bedfordshire/SouldropRollofHonour.html
  World Wars I & II

Southill

- Southill Parish Hall Memorial
  www.roll-of-honour.com/Bedfordshire/SouthillParishHallRollofHonour.html
  World Wars I & II

Stagsden

- Stagsden Roll of Honour
  www.roll-of-honour.com/Bedfordshire/StagsdenRollofHonour.html
  World Wars I & II

Steppingley

- Steppingley St. Lawrence: Roll of Honour
  www.roll-of-honour.com/Bedfordshire/SteppingleyStLawrenceRollofHonour.html
  World War I

Stevington

- Stevington Roll of Honour
  www.roll-of-honour.com/Bedfordshire/StevingtonRollofHonour.html
  World Wars I & II

Stopsley

- Stopsley War Memorial
  www.roll-of-honour.com/Bedfordshire/StopsleyRollofHonour.html
  World Wars I & II

Stotfold

- Stotfold War Memorial
  www.roll-of-honour.com/Bedfordshire/StotfoldRollofHonour.html
  World Wars I & II

Studham

- Studham: Rolls of Honour
  www.roll-of-honour.com/Bedfordshire/StudhamRollofHonour.html
  World Wars I & II

Sundon

- Sundon Village: Roll of Honour
  www.roll-of-honour.com/Bedfordshire/SundonVillageRollofHonour.html
  World Wars I & II

- Sundon Cement and Lime Works Roll of Honour
  www.roll-of-honour.com/Bedfordshire/SundonCementRollofHonour.html
  World War I

Sutton

- Sutton, All Saints Church: Roll of Honour
  www.roll-of-honour.com/Bedfordshire/SuttonRollofHonour.html
  World Wars I & II

Swineshead

- Swineshead Roll of Honour
  www.roll-of-honour.com/Bedfordshire/SwinesheadRollofHonour.html
  World Wars I & II

Tebworth

See Chalgrove

Tempsford

- Tempsford, St. Peter: Roll of Honour
  www.roll-of-honour.com/Bedfordshire/TempsfordStPeterRollofHonour.html
  World Wars I & II, & Boer War

Thurleigh

- Thurleigh War Memorial
  www.roll-of-honour.com/Bedfordshire/ThurleighRollofHonour.html
  World Wars I & II

Tingrith

- Tingrith: St. Nicholas Church: War Memorials
  www.roll-of-honour.com/Bedfordshire/TingrithRollofHonour.html
  World Wars I & II

Toddington

- Toddington, St. George: Roll of Honour
  www.roll-of-honour.com/Bedfordshire/ToddingtonStGeorgeRollofHonour.html
  World Wars I & II

- Toddington Village: Roll of Honour
  www.roll-of-honour.com/Bedfordshire/ToddingtonVillageRollofHonour.html
  World Wars I & II

Totternhoe

- Totternhoe: Roll of Honour
  www.roll-of-honour.com/Bedfordshire/TotternhoeRollofHonour.html
  World Wars I & II

Turvey

- Turvey Roll of Honour
  www.roll-of-honour.com/Bedfordshire/TurveyRollofHonour.html
  World Wars I & II

Upper Dean

- Upper Dean Roll of Honour
  www.roll-of-honour.com/Bedfordshire/UpperDeanRollofHonour.html
  World Wars I & II

Upper Gravenhurst

- Upper Gravenhurst Roll of Honour
  www.roll-of-honour.com/Bedfordshire/UpperGravenhurstRollofHonour.html
  World Wars I & II

Upper Stondon

- Upper Stondon War Memorial
  www.roll-of-honour.com/Bedfordshire/UpperStondonRollofHonour.html
  World Wars I & II

Westoning

- Westoning: Roll of Honour
  www.roll-of-honour.com/Bedfordshire/WestoningRollofHonour.html
  World Wars I & II

Whipsnade

- Whipsnade: Roll of Honour
  www.rolls-of-honour.com/Bedfordshire/WhipsnadeRollofHonour.html
  World War I

Wilden

- Wilden: Roll of Honour
  www.roll-of-honour.com/Bedfordshire/WildenRollofHonour.html
  World Wars I & II

Willington

- Willington: Village Hall: Roll of Honour
  www.roll-of-honour.com/Bedfordshire/WillingtonRollofHonour.html
  World Wars I & II

Wilshamstead

- Wilstead (Wilshamstead): Roll of Honour
  www.roll-of-honour.com/Bedfordshire/WilsteadRollofHonour.html
  World Wars I & II

Woburn

- Woburn War Memorial
  www.roll-of-honour.com/Bedfordshire/WoburnRollofHonour.html
  World War I

- Woburn Parish Church: Hospital Memorials
  www.roll-of-honour.com/Bedfordshire/WoburnHospitalRollofHonour.html
  World War I, *etc.*

Woburn Sands

- Woburn Sands: Roll of Honour
  www.roll-of-honour.com/Bedfordshire/WoburnSandsRollofHonour.html
  World War I

Woodside

See Slip End

Wootton
- Wootton Roll of Honour
  www.roll-of-honour.com/Bedfordshire/WoottonRollofHonour.html
  World Wars I & II

Wrestlingworth
- Wrestlingworth: Roll of Honour
  www.roll-of-honour.com/Bedfordshire/WrestlingworthRollofHonour.html
  World Wars I & II

Wymington
- Wymington Roll of Honour
  www.roll-of-honour.com/Bedfordshire/WymingtonRollofHonour.html
  World Wars I & II

Yelden
- Yelden: Roll of Honour
  www.roll-of-honour.com/Bedfordshire/YeldenRollofHonour.html
  World Wars I & II

Cambridgeshire

General
- Cambridgeshire War Memorials & Rolls of Honour
  www.roll-of-honour.com/Cambridgeshire/Cambridgeshire.html

- 30th Foot (Cambridgeshire) Crimean Casualties
  www.cfhs.org.uk/Crimea30thFootCasualties/
  Searchable database

- Cambridgeshire Boer War Memorial Roll of Honour and other
  information
  www.roll-of-honour.com/Cambridgeshire/BoerWarCambridge.html

- Boer War Deaths: Cambs., Hunts., & Beds
  www.cfhs.org.uk/BoerWarDeaths/
  Online database from memorials at Bedford, Cambridge, Ely,
  Huntingdon and Peterborough

Abington Pigotts
- Abington Piggots Roll of Honour
  www.roll-of-honour.com/Cambridgeshire/AbingtonPigotts.html
  World Wars I & II

Arrington
  See Wimpole

Ashley cum Silverley
- Ashley-cum-Silverley Roll of Honour
  www.roll-of-honour.com/Cambridgeshire/AshleycumSilverley.html
  World Wars I & II

Babraham
- Babraham Roll of Honour
  www.roll-of-honour.com/Cambridgeshire/Babraham.html
  World Wars I & II

Balsham
- Balsham: Roll of Honour
  www.roll-of-honour.com/Cambridgeshire/Balsham.html
  World Wars I & II, and the Boer War

Barrington

- Barrington: Roll of Honour
  www.roll-of-honour.com/Cambridgeshire/Barrington.html
  World Wars I & II

Bartlow

- Bartlow: Roll of Honour
  www.roll-of-honour.com/Cambridgeshire/Bartlow.html
  World Wars I & II

Barton

- Barton: War Memorial
  www.roll-of-honour.com/Cambridgeshire/barton.html
  World Wars I & II

Bassingbourn

- Bassingbourn-cum-Kneesworth: Roll of Honour
  www.roll-of-honour.com/Cambridgeshire/BassingbourncumKneesworth.html
  World Wars I & II

- Bassingbourn-cum-Kneesworth: R.A.F. graves
  www.roll-of-honour.com/Cambridgeshire/
  BassingbourncumKneesworthRAFGraves.html
  World War II

- Bassingbourn-cum-Kneesworth Post War Graves
  www.roll-of-honour.com/Cambridgeshire/
  BasssingbournecumKneesworthPostWar.html
  Airmen and soldiers who died at Bassingbourne base

Benwick

- Benwick: Roll of Honour
  www.roll-of-honour.com/Cambridgeshire/Benwick.html
  World Wars I & II

Bottisham

- Bottisham, Holy Trinity: Roll of Honour
  www.roll-of-honour.com/Cambridgeshire/BottishamHolyTrinity.html
  World Wars I & II

Bourn

- Bourn: Roll of Honour
  www.roll-of-honour.com/Cambridgeshire/Bourn.html
  World Wars I & II

Boxworth

- Boxworth: Roll of Honour
  www.roll-of-honour.com/Cambridgeshire/Boxworth.html
  World Wars I & II

Brinkley

- Brinkley: Roll of Honour
  www.roll-of-honour.com/Cambridgeshire/Brinkley.html
  World War I

Burrough Green

- Burrough Green: Roll of Honour
  www.roll-of-honour.com/Cambridgeshire/BurroughGreen.html
  World Wars I & II

Burwell

- Burwell War Memorial
  www.roll-of-honour.com/Cambridgeshire/burwell.html
  World Wars I & II

Caldecote

- Caldecote: Roll of Honour
  www.roll-of-honour.com/Cambridgeshire/Caldecote.html
  World Wars I & II

Cambridge

- Cambridge Guildhall
  www.roll-of-honour.com/Cambridgeshire/CambridgeGuildhall.html
  World Wars I & II. To be transcribed

- Cambridge City Crematorium Roll of Honour
  www.roll-of-honour.com/Cambridgeshire/CambridgeCrematorium.html
  World War II

- First World War Roll of Honour
  www.quns.cam.ac.uk/Queens/Record/2001/History/www1.html
  For Queens College, Cambridge University

- Second World War Roll of Honour
  www.quns.cam.ac.uk/Queens/Record/2000/History/Honour.html
  For Queens College, Cambridge University

- Cambridge All Saints
  www.roll-of-honour.com/Cambridgeshire/CambridgeAllSaints.html
  World War I

- Cambridge: Holy Sepulchre: Roll of Honour
  www.roll-of-honour.com/Cambridgeshire/CambridgeHolySepulchre.htm
  World War I

- Cambridge, Holy Trinity: Roll of Honour
  www.roll-of-honour.com/Cambridgeshire/CambridgeHolyTrinity.html
  World War I

- Cambridge, St. Andrew the Great: Roll of Honour
  www.roll-of-honour.com/Cambridgeshire/CambridgeStAtG.html
  World War I

- Cambridge St. Benets (Benedicts): Roll of Honour
  www.roll-of-honour.com/Cambridgeshire/CambridgeStBenets.html
  World War I

- Cambridge, St. Giles: Roll of Honour
  www.roll-of-honour.com/Cambridgeshire/CambridgeStGiles.html
  World War I

- Cambridge, St. Johns: Roll of Honour
  www.roll-of-honour.com/Cambridgeshire/CambridgeStJohns.html
  World Wars I & II

- Cambridge, St. Lukes: Roll of Honour
  www.roll-of-honour.com/Cambridgeshire/CambridgeStLukes.html
  World Wars I & II

- Cambridge, St. Marks
  www.roll-of-honour.com/Cambridgeshire/CambridgeStMarks.html
  World Wars I & II

- Cambridge, St. Mary the Great: Roll of Honour
  www.roll-of-honour.com/Cambridgeshire/CambridgeStMarytheGreat.html
  World Wars I & II

- Cambridge, Shire Hall: Roll of Honour
  www.roll-of-honour.com/Cambridgeshire/CambridgeShireHall.htm

Carlton
- Carlton: Roll of Honour
  www.roll-of-honour.com/Cambridgeshire/Carlton.html
  World Wars I & II

Castle Camps
- Castle Camps: Roll of Honour
  www.roll-of-honour.com/Cambridgeshire/CastleCamps.html
  World Wars I & II

- Castle Camps Roll of Honour
  www.users.globalnet.co.uk/%7Erodg/ccamps.htm
  World Wars I & II

Caxton
- Caxton: Roll of Honour
  www.roll-of-honour.com/Cambridgeshire/Caxton.html
  World Wars I & II

Chainbridge
- Chainbridge: Roll of Honour
  www.roll-of-honour.com/Cambridgeshire/Chainbridge.html
  World War I

Chatteris
- Chatteris: Roll of Honour
  www.roll-of-honour.com/Cambridgeshire/Chatteris.html
  World Wars I & II

- Chatteris War Memorial
  www.huntscycles.co.uk/Memorials/Chatteris.htm
  World War I

Cherry Hinton
- Cherry Hinton: Roll of Honour
  www.roll-of-honour.com/Cambridgeshire/CherryHinton.html
  World Wars I & II

Chesterton
- Chesterton, Arbury Church: Roll of Honour: The Chesterton
  Chapel/Arbury Church War Memorial
  www.roll-of-honour.com/Cambridgeshire/ChestertonArbury.html
  World Wars I & II

- Chesterton: Roll of Honour
  www.roll-of-honour.com/Cambridgeshire/Chesterton.html
  World wars I & II, *etc.*

Chettisham
- Ely, Chettisham: Roll of Honour
  www.roll-of-honour.com/Cambridgeshire/ElyChettisham.html
  World War I

Cheveley
- Cheveley: Roll of Honour
  www.roll-of-honour.com/Cambridgeshire/Cheveley.html
  World Wars I & II

Childerley
- Childerley: Roll of Honour
  www.roll-of-honour.com/Cambridgeshire/Childerley.html
  World War I

Chippenham
- Chippenham: Roll of Honour
  www.roll-of-honour.com/Cambridgeshire/Chippenham.html
  World Wars I & II

Christchurch
- Christchurch: Roll of Honour
  www.roll-of-honour.com/Cambridgeshire/Christchurch.html
  World Wars I & II

Clopton
See Croydon

Coates
- Coates: War Memorial
  www.roll-of-honour.com/Cambridgeshire/coates.htmL
  World Wars I & II

Coldham
- Coldham: Roll of Honour
  www.roll-of-honour.com/Cambridgeshire/Coldham.html
  World Wars I & II

Comberton
- Comberton: Roll of Honour
  www.roll-of-honour.com/Cambridgeshire/Comberton.html
  World Wars I & II

Conington
- Conington: Roll of Honour
  www.roll-of-honour.com/Cambridgeshire/Conington.html
  World War I

Coton
- Coton: Roll of Honour
  www.roll-of-honour.com/Cambridgeshire/Coton.html
  World War I

Cottenham
- Cottenham: War Memorial
  www.roll-of-honour.com/Cambridgeshire/Cottenham.html
  World Wars I & II; also India 1857

Coveney
- Coveney: Roll of Honour
  www.roll-of-honour.com/Cambridgeshire/Coveney.html
  World War I

Croxton
- Croxton: Roll of Honour
  www.roll-of-honour.com/Cambridgeshire/Croxton.html
  World Wars I & II

Croydon
- Croydon cum Clopton: War Memorial
  www.roll-of-honour.com/Cambridgeshire/CroydoncumClopton.html
  World War I

Doddington
- Doddington: War Memorial
  www.roll-of-honour.com/Cambridgeshire/Doddington.html
  World Wars I & II; also Boer War
- Doddington School War Memorial
  www.roll-of-honour.com/Cambridgeshire/DoddingtonSchoolWar.html
  World War I

Dry Drayton
- Dry Drayton: Roll of Honour
  www.roll-of-honour.com/Cambridgeshire/DryDrayton.html
  World Wars I & II

Dullingham
- Dullingham: Roll of Honour
  www.roll-of-honour.com/Cambridgeshire/Dullingham.html
  World Wars I & II

Duxford
- Duxford: Roll of Honour
  www.roll-of-honour.com/Cambridgeshire/Duxford.html
  World Wars I & II

East Hatley
- East Hatley & Hatley St. George: Roll of Honour
  www.roll-of-honour.com/Cambridgeshire/Hatleys.html
  World Wars I & II

Eastrea
- Eastrea: Roll of Honour
  www.roll-of-honour.com/Cambridgeshire/Eastrea.html
  World Wars I & II

Elm
- Elm: Roll of Honour
  www.roll-of-honour.com/Cambridgeshire/Elm.html
  World Wars I & II

Elsworth
- Elsworth: Roll of Honour
  www.roll-of-honour.com/Cambridgeshire/Elsworth.html
  World Wars I & II

Eltisley
- Eltisley: Roll of Honour
  www.roll-of-honour.com/Cambridgeshire/Eltisley.html
  World Wars I & II

- Eltisley War Memorial
  www.huntscycles.co.uk/Memorials/Eltisley.htm
  World War I

Ely
- Cambridgeshire: Ely Cathedral Boer War Memorial: Roll of Honour
  and other information
  www.roll-of-honour.com/Cambridgeshire/ElyBoerWar.html

- Ely World War I: Roll of Honour
  www.roll-of-honour.com/Cambridgeshire/ElyWorldWar1.html

- Ely World War II: Roll of Honour
  www.roll-of-honour.com/Cambridgeshire/ElyWorldWar2.html

- Ely Holy Trinity: Roll of Honour
  www.roll-of-honour.com/Cambridgeshire/ElyHolyTrinity.html
  World War I

- Ely Queen Adelaide: Roll of Honour
  www.roll-of-honour.com/Cambridgeshire/ElyQueenAdelaide.html
  World War I

- Ely: Cemetery: Graves
  www.roll-of-honour.com/Cambridgeshire/ElyCemetery.html
  Boer War, World Wars I & II, *etc.*

Fen Ditton
- Fen Ditton: Roll of Honour
  www.roll-of-honour.com/Cambridgeshire/FenDitton.html
  World Wars I & II

Fen Drayton
- Fen Drayton: War Memorial
  www.roll-of-honour.com/Cambridgeshire/fendrayton.html
  World Wars I & II

Fordham
- Fordham: Roll of Honour
  www.roll-of-honour.com/Cambridgeshire/Fordham.html
  World Wars I & II

Foulanchor
- Foulanchor: Roll of Honour
  www.roll-of-honour.com/Cambridgeshire/Foulanchor.html
  World War I

Fowlmere

- Fowlmere: Roll of Honour
  www.roll-of-honour.com/Cambridgeshire/Fowlmere.html
  World Wars I & II

Foxton

- Foxton: Roll of Honour
  www.roll-of-honour.com/Cambridgeshire/Foxton.html
  World Wars I & II

Friday Bridge

- Friday Bridge: Roll of Honour
  www.roll-of-honour.com/Cambridgeshire/FridayBridge.html
  World Wars I & II

Fulbourn

- Fulbourn: Roll of Honour
  www.roll-of-honour.com/Cambridgeshire/Fulbourn.html
  World Wars I & II, Gulf War, *etc.*

Gamlingay

- Gamlingay: Roll of Honour
  www.roll-of-honour.com/Cambridgeshire/Gamlingay.html
  World Wars I & II

Gamlingay Heath

- Cambridgeshire: Gamlingay Heath & Tetworth: Roll of Honour
  www.roll-of-honour.com/Cambridgeshire/Memorials/
  GamlingayHeathTetworth.html
  World Wars I & II

Girton

- Girton: Roll of Honour
  www.roll-of-honour.com/Cambridgeshire/Girton.html
  World Wars I & II

Gorefield

- Gorefield: Roll of Honour
  www.roll-of-honour.com/Cambridgeshire/Gorefield.html
  World Wars I & II

Grantchester

- Grantchester: Roll of Honour
  www.roll-of-honour.com/Cambridgeshire/Grantchester.html
  World Wars I & II

Graveley

- Graveley War Memorials:
  www.roll-of-honour.com/Cambridgeshire/Graveley.html
  World Wars I & II

Great Abington

- Great Abington: Roll of Honour
  www.roll-of-honour.com/Cambridgeshire/GreatAbington.html
  World Wars I & II

Great Eversden

- The Eversdens, Great & Little: Roll of Honour
  www.roll-of-honour.com/Cambridgeshire/Eversdens.html
  World Wars I & II

Great Shelford

- Great Shelford: Roll of Honour
  www.roll-of-honour.com/Cambridgeshire/GreatShelford.html
  World Wars I & II

- Great Shelford St. Mary: Roll of Honour
  www.roll-of-honour.com/Cambridgeshire/GreatShelfordStMary.html
  World Wars I & II

- Great Shelford Village Hall: Roll of Honour
  www.roll-of-honour.com/Cambridgeshire/GreatShelfordVillageHall.html
  Word Wars I & II

Great Wilbraham

- Great Wilbraham, St Nicholas: Roll of Honour
  www.roll-of-honour.com/Cambridgeshire/GreatWilbraham.html
  World Wars I & II

Guilden Morden

- Guilden Morden: Roll of Honour
  www.roll-of-honour.com/Cambridgeshire/GuildenMorden.html
  World Wars I & II

Guyhirn

- Guyhirn and Ring's End: Roll of Honour
  www.roll-of-honour.com/Cambridgeshire/GuyhirnRingsEnd.html
  World Wars I & II

Haddenham

- Haddenham: Roll of Honour
  www.roll-of-honour.com/Cambridgeshire/Haddenham.html
  World Wars I & II

Hardwick

- Hardwick: Roll of Honour
  www.roll-of-honour.com/Cambridgeshire/Hardwick.html
  World Wars I & II

Harlton

- Harlton: Roll of Honour
  www.roll-of-honour.com/Cambridgeshire/Harlton.html
  World War I

- Harlton St Mary: Roll of Honour 1914-1918
  www.roll-of-honour.com/Cambridgeshire/HarltonStMary.html
  World War I

Harston

- Harston: Roll of Honour
  www.roll-of-honour.com/Cambridgeshire/Harston.html
  World Wars I & II

Haslingfield

- Haslingfield: Roll of Honour
  www.roll-of-honour.com/Cambridgeshire/Haslingfield.html
  World Wars I & II

Hatley St George
  See East Hatley

Hauxton

- Hauxton: Roll of Honour
  www.roll-of-honour.com/Cambridgeshire/Hauxton.html
  World Wars I & II

Hildersham

- Hildersham: Roll of Honour
  www.roll-of-honour.com/Cambridgeshire/Hildersham.html
  World Wars I & II

Hinxton

- Hinxton: Roll of Honour
  www.roll-of-honour.com/Cambridgeshire/Hinxton.html
  World Wars I & II

Histon

- Histon and Impington: War Memorial
  www.roll-of-honour.com/Cambridgeshire/histonandimpington.html
  World Wars I & II

- Histon Methodist: Roll of Honour
  www.roll-of-honour.com/Cambridgeshire/HistonMethodist.html
  World Wars I & II

Horningsea

- Horningsea: Roll of Honour
  www.roll-of-honour.com/Cambridgeshire/Horningsea.html
  World Wars I & II

Horseheath

- Horseheath: Roll of Honour
  www.roll-of-honour.com/Cambridgeshire/Horseheath.html
  World Wars I & II

Ickleton

- Ickleton: Roll of Honour
  www.roll-of-honour.com/Cambridgeshire/Ickleton.html
  World Wars I & II

Impington

- Impington St Andrew: Roll of Honour
  www.roll-of-honour.com/Cambridgeshire/ImpingtonStAndrew.html
  World Wars I & II
  See also Histon

Isleham
- Isleham: Roll of Honour
  www.roll-of-honour.com/Cambridgeshire/Isleham.html
  World Wars I & II

Kennett
- Kennett: Roll of Honour
  www.roll-of-honour.com/Cambridgeshire/Kennett.html
  World Wars I & II

Kingston
- Kingston: Roll of Honour
  www.roll-of-honour.com/Cambridgeshire/Kingston.html
  World Wars I & II

Kirtling
- Kirtling: Roll of Honour
  www.roll-of-honour.com/Cambridgeshire/Kirtling.html
  World Wars I & II

Knapwell
- Knapwell: Roll of Honour
  www.roll-of-honour.com/Cambridgeshire/Knapwell.html
  World War II

Kneesworth
  See Bassingbourne

Landbeach
- Landbeach: Roll of Honour
  www.roll-of-honour.com/Cambridgeshire/landbeach.html
  World Wars I & II

Leverington
- Leverington: Roll of Honour
  www.roll-of-honour.com/Cambridgeshire/Leverington.html
  World Wars I & II

Linton
- Linton: Roll of Honour
  www.roll-of-honour.com/Cambridgeshire/Linton.html
  World Wars I & II

- Linton St Mary: Roll of Honour
  www.roll-of-honour.com/Cambridgeshire/LintonStMary.html
  World Wars I & II

Litlington
- Litlington: Roll of Honour
  www.roll-of-honour.com/Cambridgeshire/Litlington.html
  World Wars I & II

Little Abington
- Little Abington: Roll of Honour
  www.roll-of-honour.com/Cambridgeshire/LittleAbington.html
  World Wars I & II

Little Downham
- Little Downham: Roll of Honour
  www.roll-of-honour.com/Cambridgeshire/LittleDownham.html
  World Wars I & II

Little Eversden
  See Great Eversden

Little Gransden
- Little Gransden: Roll of Honour
  www.roll-of-honour.com/Cambridgeshire/LittleGransden.html
  World Wars I & II

Little Ouse
- Little Ouse, Littleport: Roll of Honour
  www.roll-of-honour.com/Cambridgeshire/LittleOuse.html
  World War I

Little Shelford
- Little Shelford All Saints Church: Roll of Honour
  www.roll-of-honour.com/Cambridgeshire/LittleShelfordAllSaints.html
  World Wars I & II

- Little Shelford Congregational Church: Roll of Honour
  www.roll-of-honour.com/Cambridgeshire/LittleShelfordCongregational.html
  World War I

Little Thetford

- Little Thetford: Roll of Honour
  www.roll-of-honour.com/Cambridgeshire/LittleThetford.html
  World Wars I & II, *etc.*

Little Wilbraham

- Little Wilbraham, St. John: Roll of Honour
  www.roll-of-honour.com/Cambridgeshire/LittleWilbrahamStJohn.html
  World Wars I & II

Littleport

- Littleport: Roll of Honour
  www.roll-of-honour.com/Cambridgeshire/Littleport.html
  World Wars I & II

- Littleport St. Matthews: Roll of Honour
  www.roll-of-honour.com/Cambridgeshire/LittleportStMatthews.html
  World Wars I & II

Lode

- Lode: War Memorial
  www.roll-of-honour.com/Cambridgeshire/lode.html
  World Wars I & II Roll of Honour

Lolworth

- Lolworth: Roll of Honour
  www.roll-of-honour.com/Cambridgeshire/Lolworth.html
  World War I

Longstanton

- Longstanton: War Memorial
  www.roll-of-honour.com/Cambridgeshire/longstanton.html
  World Wars I & II, *etc.*

Longstowe

- Longstowe: Roll of Honour
  www.roll-of-honour.com/Cambridgeshire/Longstowe.html
  World Wars I & II

Madingley

- Madingley St Mary Magdalene 19th century memorials
  www.roll-of-honour.com/Cambridgeshire/
  MadingleyStMaryMagdalene19thCentury.html

  Military memorials

Madingley St Mary Magdalene: War Memorials
  www.roll-of-honour.com/Cambridgeshire/MadingleyStMaryMagdalene.html
  World Wars I & II

Manea

- Manea: Roll of Honour
  www.roll-of-honour.com/Cambridgeshire/Manea.html
  World Wars I & II

March

- March: Roll of Honour
  www.roll-of-honour.com/Cambridgeshire/March.html
  World Wars I & II, *etc.*

- March: Isle of Ely County Council: Roll of Honour
  www.roll-of-honour.com/Cambridgeshire/MarchIofECountyCouncil.html
  World War II

- March Grammar School Old Boys: Roll of Honour
  www.roll-of-honour.com/Cambridgeshire/MarchGrammarSchool.html
  World Wars I & II

- March St. Wendreda's: Doddington Yeomanry
  www.roll-of-honour.com/Cambridgeshire/marchstwendreda.html
  Roll of honour, 1798 and 1827

- March War Memorial
  www.huntscycles.co.uk/Memorials/March.htm
  Forthcoming

Melbourn

- Melbourn: Roll of Honour
  www.roll-of-honour.com/Cambridgeshire/Melbourn.html
  World Wars I & II

- Melbourn All Saints: Roll of Honour
  www.roll-of-honour.com/Cambridgeshire/MelbournAllSaints.html
  World War I

Meldreth

- Meldreth: Roll of Honour
  www.roll-of-honour.com/Cambridgeshire/Meldreth.html
  World Wars I & II

- Meldreth Holy Trinity: Roll of Honour
  www.roll-of-honour.com/Cambridgeshire/MeldrethHolyTrinity.html
  World Wars I & II

Mepal
- Mepal: Roll of Honour
  www.roll-of-honour.com/Cambridgeshire/Mepal.html
  World Wars I & II

Milton
- Milton: Roll of Honour
  www.roll-of-honour.com/Cambridgeshire/Milton.html
  World Wars I & II

Murrow
- Murrow: Roll of Honour
  www.roll-of-honour.com/Cambridgeshire/Murrow.html
  World War I

Newton
- Newton, Cambridge: Roll of Honour
  www.roll-of-honour.com/Cambridgeshire/NewtonCambridge.html
  World Wars I & II

Newton in the Isle
- Newton-in-the-Isle: Roll of Honour
  www.roll-of-honour.com/Cambridgeshire/Newtoninthelsle.html
  World Wars I & II

Oakington
- Oakington St Andrew: Roll of Honour
  www.roll-of-honour.com/Cambridgeshire/OakingtonStAndrew.html

Orwell
- Orwell St Andrew: Roll of Honour
  www.roll-of-honour.com/Cambridgeshire/OrwellStAndrew.html
  World Wars I & II

Outwell
- Outwell: Roll of Honour
  www.roll-of-honour.com/Cambridgeshire/Outwell.html
  World Wars I & II

Over
- Over: War Memorial
  www.roll-of-honour.com/Cambridgeshire/over.html
  World Wars I & II

- Over St Mary: Roll of Honour
  www.roll-of-honour.com/Cambridgeshire/OverStMary.html
  World Wars I & II

Pampisford
- Pampisford St John the Baptist: Roll of Honour
  www.roll-of-honour.com/Cambridgeshire/PampisfordStJohntheBaptist.html
  World Wars I & II

Papworth Agnes
- Papworth Agnes: Roll of Honour
  www.roll-of-honour.com/Cambridgeshire/PapworthStAgnes.html
  World Wars I & II

Papworth Everard
- Papworth Everard: Roll of Honour
  www.roll-of-honour.com/Cambridgeshire/PapworthEverard.html
  World Wars I & II

Parson Drove
- Parson Drove: Roll of Honour
  www.roll-of-honour.com/Cambridgeshire/ParsonDrove.html

Prickwillow
- Ely, Prickwillow: War Memorial
  www.roll-of-honour.com/Cambridgeshire/elyprickwillow.html
  World Wars I & II

Rampton
- Rampton: Roll of Honour
  www.roll-of-honour.com/Cambridgeshire/Rampton.html
  World War I & II

Reach
- Cambridgeshire, Reach: Roll of Honour
  www.roll-of-honour.com/Cambridgeshire/Reach.html
  World War I

Redmere

- Redmere (Littleport): Roll of Honour
  www.roll-of-honour.com/Cambridgeshire/Redmere.html
  World War I

Rings End

See Guyhirn

Sawston

- Sawston: Roll of Honour
  www.roll-of-honour.com/Cambridgeshire/Sawston.html
  World Wars I & II, and the Korean War

- Sawston St Mary: Roll of Honour
  www.roll-of-honour.com/Cambridgeshire/SawstonStMary.html
  World Wars I & II, and the Korean War

- Sawston Village College: Roll of Honour
  www.roll-of-honour.com/Cambridgeshire/SawstonVillageCollege.html
  World War II

Saxon Street

- Saxon Street: Roll of Honour
  www.roll-of-honour.com/Cambridgeshire/SaxonStreet.html

Shepreth

- Shepreth: Roll of Honour
  www.roll-of-honour.com/Cambridgeshire/Shepreth.html
  World Wars I & II

Shudy Camps

- Shudy Camps: Roll of Honour
  www.roll-of-honour.com/Cambridgeshire/ShudyCamps.html
  World Wars I & II

Six Mile Bottom

- Six Mile Bottom: Roll of Honour
  www.roll-of-honour.com/Cambridgeshire/SixMileBottom.html
  World War I

Snailwell

- Snailwell: Roll of Honour
  www.roll-of-honour.com/Cambridgeshire/Snailwell.html
  World Wars I & II

Soham

- Soham: Roll of Honour
  www.roll-of-honour.com/Cambridgeshire/Soham.html
  World Wars I & II

- Soham Grammar School: Roll of Honour
  www.roll-of-honour.com/Cambridgeshire/SohamGrammarSchool.html
  World War I

Stapleford

- Stapleford: Roll of Honour
  www.roll-of-honour.com/Cambridgeshire/Stapleford.html
  World Wars I & II

Steeple Morden

- Steeple Morden: Roll of Honour
  www.roll-of-honour.com/Cambridgeshire/SteepleMorden.html
  World Wars I & II

Stetchworth

- Stetchworth: Roll of Honour
  www.roll-of-honour.com/Cambridgeshire/Stetchworth.html
  World Wars I & II

Stow cum Quy

- Stow-cum-Quy: Roll of Honour
  www.roll-of-honour.com/Cambridgeshire/StowCumQuy.html
  World Wars I & II

Stretham

- Stretham: Roll of Honour
  www.roll-of-honour.com/Cambridgeshire/Stretham.html
  World Wars I & II

Stuntney

- Ely Stuntney: Roll of Honour
  www.roll-of-honour.com/Cambridgeshire/ElyStuntney.html
  World Wars I & II

Sutton

- Sutton: Roll of Honour
  www.roll-of-honour.com/Cambridgeshire/sutton.html
  World Wars I & II

Swaffham Bulbeck

- Swaffham Bulbeck: War Memorial
  www.roll-of-honour.com/Cambridgeshire/SwaffhamBulbeck.html
  World Wars I & II

Swaffham Fen

- Swaffham Fen Methodist Memorial
  www.roll-of-honour.com/Cambridgeshire/SwaffhamFenMethodist.html
  World War I

Swaffham Prior

- Swaffham Prior St Mary: Roll of Honour
  www.roll-of-honour.com/Cambridgeshire/SwaffhamPriorStMary.html
  World Wars I & II

- Swaffham Prior Zion Church
  www.roll-of-honour.com/Cambridgeshire/SwaffhamPriorZion.html
  World War I

Swavesey

- The Swavesey Chronicles: the story of a Fenland Village during the 1914-1918 War
  www.curme.co.uk/swavgw1.htm
  Includes roll of honour

- Swavesey War Memorial Hall: Roll of Honour
  www.roll-of-honour.com/Cambridgeshire/Swavesey.html
  World War I

- Swavesey St. Andrew: Roll of Honour
  www.roll-of-honour.com/Cambridgeshire/Swavesey/StAndrew.html
  World Wars I & II, and Falklands War

Tadlow

- Tadlow: Roll of Honour
  www.roll-of-honour.com/Cambridgeshire/Tadlow.html
  World War I

Tetworth

    See Gamlingay Heath

Teversham

- Teversham: Roll of Honour
  www.roll-of-honour.com/Cambridgeshire/Teversham.html
  World Wars I & II

Thorney

- Thorney: Roll of Honour
  www.roll-of-honour.com/Cambridgeshire/Thorney.html
  World Wars I & II

Thriplow

- Thriplow: Roll of Honour
  www.roll-of-honour.com/Cambridgeshire/Thriplow.html
  World Wars I & II

- Thriplow Memorial
  www.thriplow.com/thriplow__memorial.htm

Toft

- Toft: Roll of Honour
  www.roll-of-honour.com/Cambridgeshire/ToftMethodist.html
  World War II

Trumpington

- Trumpington: War Memorial
  www.roll-of-honour.com/Cambridgeshire/Trumpington.html
  World Wars I & II

Turves

- Turves: War Memorial
  www.roll-of-honour.com/Cambridgeshire/Turves.html
  World War I

Tydd St. Giles

- Tydd St Giles: Roll of Honour
  www.roll-of-honour.com/Cambridgeshire/TyddStGiles.html
  World Wars I & II, *etc.*

Upwell
- Upwell: Roll of Honour
  www.roll-of-honour.com/Cambridgeshire/Upwell.html
  World Wars I & II

Waterbeach
- Waterbeach: War Memorial
  www.roll-of-honour.com/Cambridgeshire/waterbeach.html
  World Wars I & II

- Waterbeach St John: Roll of Honour
  www.roll-of-honour.com/Cambridgeshire/WaterbeachStJohn.html
  World War I

Wendy with Shingay
- Wendy-cum-Shingay: Roll of Honour
  www.roll-of-honour.com/Cambridgeshire/WendycumShingay.html
  World Wars I & II

Wentworth
- Wentworth: Roll of Honour
  www.roll-of-honour.com/Cambridgeshire/Wentworth.html
  World War I

West Wickham
- West Wickham: Roll of Honour
  www.roll-of-honour.com/Cambridgeshire/WestWickham.html
  World Wars I & II

West Wratting
- West Wratting: Roll of Honour
  www.roll-of-honour.com/Cambridgeshire/WestWratting.html
  World War I

Westley Waterless
- Westley Waterless: Roll of Honour
  www.roll-of-honour.com/Cambridgeshire/WestleyWaterless.html
  World Wars I & II

Weston Colville
- Weston Colville: Roll of Honour
  www.roll-of-honour.com/Cambridgeshire/WestonColville.html
  World War I

Whaddon
- Whaddon: Roll of Honour
  www.roll-of-honour.com/Cambridgeshire/Whaddon.html
  World Wars I & II

Whittlesey
- Whittlesey: Roll of Honour
  www.roll-of-honour.com/Cambridgeshire/Whittlesey.html
  World Wars I & II

- Whittlesey War Memorial
  www.huntscycles.co.uk/Memorials/Whittlesey.htm
  World War I

Whittlesford
- Whittlesford: Roll of Honour
  www.roll-of-honour.com/Cambridgeshire/Whittlesford.html
  World Wars I & II

Wicken
- Wicken: Roll of Honour
  www.roll-of-honour.com/Cambridgeshire/Wicken.html
  World Wars I & II

Wilburton
- Wilburton War Memorial
  www.roll-of-honour.com/Cambridgeshire/wilburton.html
  World War I

Willingham
- Willingham: Roll of Honour
  www.roll-of-honour.com/Cambridgeshire/willingham.html
  World Wars I & II

Wimblington
- Wimblington: Roll of Honour
  www.roll-of-honour.com/Cambridgeshire/Wimblington.html
  World Wars I & II, *etc.*

Wimpole
- Wimpole and Arrington War Memorial
  www.wimpole.uk.com/memorial.htm

- Wimpole and Arrington: Roll of Honour
  www.roll-of-honour.com/Cambridgeshire/WimpoleArrington.html
  World Wars I & II

Wisbech

- Wisbech 1914-1918: Roll of Honour
  www.roll-of-honour.com/Cambridgeshire/Wisbech1914-19.html

- Wisbech 1939-45: Roll of Honour
  www.roll-of-honour.com/Cambridgeshire/Wisbech1939-45.html

- Wisbech Grammar School: Roll of Honour
  www.roll-of-honour.com/Cambridgeshire/WisbechGrammarSchool.html
  World War I

- Wisbech Isle of Ely Constabulary: Roll of Honour
  www.roll-of-honour.com/Cambridgeshire/WisbechIoEConstabulary.html
  World Wars I & II

- Wisbech, Old Bartonians: Roll of Honour
  www.roll-of-honour.com/Cambridgeshire/WisbechOldBartonians.html
  World War I

- Wisbech Post Office: Roll of Honour
  www.roll-of-honour.com/Cambridgeshire/WisbechPostOffice.html
  World Wars I & II

- Wisbech, The Queen's School: Roll of Honour
  www.roll-of-honour.com/Cambridgeshire/WisbechQueensSchool.html
  World War II

- Wisbech St Mary: Roll of Honour
  www.roll-of-honour.com/Cambridgeshire/WisbechStMary.html
  World Wars I & II

Witcham

- Witcham: Roll of Honour
  www.roll-of-honour.com/Cambridgeshire/Witcham.html
  World Wars I & II

Witchford

- Witchford: Roll of Honour
  www.roll-of-honour.com/Cambridgeshire/Witchford.html
  World Wars I & II

Wood Ditton

- Woodditton: Roll of Honour
  www.roll-of-honour.com/Cambridgeshire/Woodditton.html
  World Wars I & II

Cheshire

General

- Carl's Cam: War Memorials
  www.carlscam.com/memo.html
  Collection of Cheshire war memorials separately listed below

- The Railway Volunteers: the 2nd Cheshire Royal Engineers
  www.nhannan.freeserve.co.uk/rail1.htm
  Includes Boer War roll of honour

Acton

- War Memorial, Acton, Cheshire
  www.carlscam.com/warmem/acton.htm

Alderley Edge

- Carl's Cam Memorials: War Memorial, Alderley Edge, Cheshire
  www.carlscam.com/alderley/warmem.htm
  World Wars I & II

Aldersey Green

- Carl's Cam Memorials: War Memorial, Aldersey Green, Cheshire
  www.carlscam.com/warmem/aldersey.htm
  World War I

Aldford

- Carl's Cam Memorials: War Memorial, Aldford, Cheshire
  www.carlscam.com/warmem/aldford.htm
  World War I

Alpraham

- Carl's Cam Memorials: War Memorial, Alpraham, Cheshire
  www.carlscam.com/warmem/alpraham.htm

Alsager

- Carl's Cam Memorials: War Memorial, Alsager, Cheshire
  www.carlscam.com/warmem/alsager.htm
  World Wars I & II

Altrincham

- Carl's Cam Memorials: War Memorial, Altrincham, Cheshire
  www.carlscam.com/warmem/altrincham.htm
  World Wars I & II

- Carl's Cam Memorials: War Memorial, Chapel St., Altrincham, Cheshire
  www.carlscam.com/warmem/altrincham.htm

Alvanley

- Carl's Cam Memorials: War Memorial, Alvanley, Cheshire
  www.carlscam.com/warmem/alvanley.htm
  World Wars I & II

Appleton Thorn

- Carl's Cam Memorials: War Memorial, Appleton Thorn, Cheshire
  www.carlscam.com/warmem/athorn.htm
  World Wars I & II

Ashton

- Carl's Cam Memorials: War Memorial, Ashton, Cheshire
  www.carlscam.com/warmem/ashton.htm
  World Wars I & II

Ashton upon Mersey

- Carl's Cam Memorials: War Memorial, Ashton-upon-Mersey, Cheshire
  www.carlscam.com/warmem/ashtonm.htm
  World Wars I & II

Astbury

- Carl's Cam Memorials: War Memorial, Astbury, Cheshire
  www.carlscam.com/warmem/astbury.htm
  World Wars I & II

Aston

- Carl's Cam Memorials: War Memorial, Aston, Cheshire
  www.carlscam.com/warmem/aston.htm
  World War I

Audlem

- Carl's Cam Memorials: War Memorial, Audlem, Cheshire
  www.carlscam.com/warmem/audlem.htm
  World Wars I & II

Bickerton

- Carl's Cam Memorials: War Memorial, Bickerton, Cheshire
  www.carlscam.com/warmem/bickerton.htm
  World Wars I & II

Bickley

- Carl's Cam Memorials: War Memorial, Bickley, Cheshire
  www.carlscam.com/warmem/bickley.htm
  World Wars I & II

Bidston

- Carl's Cam Memorials: War Memorial, Bidston, Cheshire
  www.carlscam.com/warmem/bidston.htm
  World War I

Birkenhead

- Carl's Cam Memorials: W.W.I. War Memorial, Birkenhead, Cheshire
  www.carlscam.com/warmem/birkenhead.htm
  World War I

- Carl's Cam Memorials: W.W.2. War Memorial, Birkenhead, Cheshire
  www.carlscam.com/warmem/birkenhed.htm

- Carl's Cam Memorials: The Thetis Memorial, Birkenhead, Cheshire
  www.carlscam.com/warmem/thetis.htm
  1939 submarine loss

Bollington

- Carl's Cam Memorials: War Memorial, Bollington, Cheshire
  www.carlscam.com/bollington/warmem.htm
  World Wars I & II

Bosley

- Carl's Cam Memorials: War Memorial, Bosley, Cheshire
  www.carlscam.com/warmem/bosley.htm
  World War I

Bowdon

- Carl's Cam Memorials: War Memorial, Bowdon, Cheshire
  www.carlscam.com/bosley/warmem.htm

Bradfield Green

- War memorial, Bradfield Green, Cheshire
  www.carlscam.com/warmem/bradfield.htm

Bramhall

- Carl's Cam Memorials: War Memorial, Bramhall, Cheshire
  www.carlscam.com/bramhall/warmem.htm
  World Wars I & II

Bredbury

- Carl's Cam Memorials: War Memorial, Bredbury and Romiley, Cheshire
  www.carlscam.com/Romiley/warmem.htm
  World Wars I & II

Brereton

- Carl's Cam Memorials: War Memorial, Brereton, Cheshire
  www.carlscam.com/warmem/brereton.htm

Broadbottom

- Carl's Cam Memorials: War Memorial, Broadbottom, Cheshire
  www.carlscam.com/broadbottom/warmem.htm
  World Wars I & II

Broken Cross

See Henbury

Bromborough

- Carl's Cam Memorials: War Memorial, Bromborough, Cheshire
  www.carlscam.com/bromborough/warmem.htm
  World Wars I & II

Bromborough Pool

- Carl's Cam Memorials: Bromborough Pool War Memorial
  www.carlscam.com/warmem/bromboroughp.htm
  World Wars I & II

Brown Knowl

- Carl's Cam War Memorials: War Memorial, Brown Knowl, Cheshire
  www.carlscam.com/warmem/brownknowl.htm
  World Wars I & II

Buglawton

- Carl's Cam Memorials: War Memorial, Buglawton, Cheshire
  www.carlscam.com/buglaw/warmem.htm
  World Wars I & II, *etc.*

Bunbury

- Carl's Cam Memorials: War Memorial, Bunbury, Cheshire
  www.carlscam.com/warmem/bunbury.htm
  World Wars I & II

Burleydam

- Carl's Cam Memorials: War Memorial, Burleydam, Cheshire
  www.carlscam.com/warmem/burleydam.htm
  World War I

Burton

- Carl's Cam Memorials: Burton Cross, Burton, Cheshire
  www.carlscam.com/warmem/burton.htm

Cheadle

- Carl's Cam Memorials: War Memorial, Cheadle, Cheshire
  www.carlscam.com/cheadle/warmem.htm
  World Wars I & II

Cheadle Hulme
- Carl's Cam Memorials: War Memorial, Cheadle Hulme, Cheshire
  www.carlscam.com/cheadlehulme/warmem.htm
  World Wars I & II

Chester
- Chester Area War Memorials
  www.users.globalnet.co.uk/~pardos/WMIndex.html
  Collection of transcripts, separately listed here

- Chester: St. Peter's Church
  www.users.globalnet.co.uk/~pardos/ChesterStP.html
  War Memorial

- Boer War Memorial, Chester Cathedral
  www.geocities.com/Heartland/Hearth/1094/BoerWarChester.html

- Memorial, India, 1843, Chester Cathedral, Chester
  www.carlscam.com/warmem/india.htm

- Memorial, Burma 1887-1890, Chester Cathedral, Cheshire
  www.carlscam.com/warmem/cheshreg.htm

- Memorial, South Africa 1899-1902, Chester Cathedral, Cheshire
  www.carlscam.com/boer/chester.htm

- Post Office Memorial
  www.users.globalnet.co.uk/~pardos/PO.html
  In Chester Post Office: war memorial

- Arnold House School Memorial Window
  www.users.globalnet.co.uk/~pardos/ArnoldHouse.html
  In Chester Cathedral: war memorial, 1914-19

- Carl's Cam Memorials: War Memorial, Town Hall, Chester, Cheshire
  www.carlscam.com/warmem/chester.htm
  World War I

- Carl's Cam Memorials: H.M.S. Chester Memorial
  www.carlscam.com/warmem/jutland.htm
  Memorial to those lost in the Battle of Jutland, 1916, in Chester Cathedral

- Carl's Cam Memorials: War Memorial to the Cheshire Brigade of the RFA Territorials
  www.carlscam.com/warmem/rfa.htm
  Click on title. World War I memorial in Chester Cathedral

- Carl's Cam Memorials: Cheshire Yeomanry War Memorial
  www.carlscam.com/warmem/yeoman.htm
  World Wars I & II memorials in Chester Cathedral

- Carl's Cam Memorials: Memorial, Northern Ireland, Chester Cathedral, Chester
  www.carlscam.com/warmem/nireland.htm
  Memorial to those who have lost their lives in Northern Ireland, mainly 1974-82

Childer Thornton
- Carl's Cam Memorials: War Memorial, Childer Thornton, Cheshire
  www.carlscam.com/warmem/lsutton.htm
  World War I & II *etc.*

Christleton
- Carl's Cam Memorials: War Memorial, Christleton, Cheshire
  www.carlscam.com/warmem/christleton.htm
  World War I

Church Minshull
- Carl's Cam Memorials: War Memorial, Church Minshull, Cheshire
  www.carlscam.com/warmem/cminshull.htm
  World Wars I & II

Comberbach
- Carl's Cam Memorials: War Memorial, Comberbach, Cheshire
  www.carlscam.com/warmem/comberbach.htm
  World Wars I & II

Compstall
- Carl's Cam Memorials: War Memorial, Compstall, Cheshire
  www.carlscam.com/compstall/warmem.htm
  World War I

Congleton
- Carl's Cam Memorials: War Memorial, Congleton, Cheshire
  www.carlscam.com/congleton/warmem.htm
  World Wars I & II

Coppenhall
- War Memorial, Coppenhall, Cheshire
  www.carlscam.com/warmem/coppenhall.htm
  World Wars I & II

Crewe
- War Memorial, Crew, Cheshire
  www.carlscam.com/warmem/crewe.htm
  World Wars I & II

- Carl's Cam Memorials: War Memorial Tranship Shed, Crewe, Cheshire
  www.carlscam.com/warmem/crewets.htm
  World Wars I & II

Crowton
- Carl's Cam Memorials: War Memorial, Crowton, Cheshire
  www.carlscam.com/warmem/crowton.htm
  World Wars I & II

Daresbury
- Carl's Cam Memorials: War Memorial, Daresbury, Cheshire
  www.carlscam.com.warmem/daresbury.htm
  World Wars I & II

Davenham
- Carl's Cam Memorials: War Memorial, Davenham, Cheshire
  www.carlscam.com/warmem/davenham.htm
  World Wars I & II

Davenport
  See Swettenham

Disley
- Carl's Cam Memorials: War Memorial, Disley, Cheshire
  www.carlscam.com/disley/warmem.htm
  World Wars I & II, *etc.*

Dukinfield
- Carl's Cam Memorials: War Memorial, St. Mark's Church, Dukinfield, Cheshire
  www.carlscam.com/dukinfield/markmem.htm
  World Wars I & II

- Carl's Cam Memorials: War Memorial, Crescent Rd., Dukinfield
  www.carlscam.com/dukinfield/memorial.htm
  World War I

- Carl's Cam Memorials: Globe Square War Memorial
  www.carlscam.com/dukinfield/globemem.htm
  In Dukinfield. World Wars I & II

- Carl's Cam Memorials: Dukinfield, Park Road, War Memorial
  www.carlscam.com/dukinfield/parkmem.htm
  World Wars I & II

Dunham Massey
- Carl's Cam Memorials: War Memorial, Dunham Town, Cheshire
  www.carlscam.com/altrincham/dunham.htm
  World Wars I & II

Eastham
- Carl's Cam Memorials: War Memorial, Eastham, Cheshire
  www.carlscam.com/warmem/eastham.htm
  World Wars I & II

Eaton
- Carl's Cam Memorials: War Memorial, Eaton, Cheshire
  www.carlscam.com/eaton/warmem.htm
  World Wars I & II

Ellesmere Port
- Carl's Cam Memorials: War Memorial, Ellesmere Port, Cheshire
  www.carlscam.com/warmem/ellesmere.htm
  World Wars I & II

Elworth
- Carls Cam Memorials: Elworth War Memorial
  www.carlscam.com/warmem/elworth.htm
  World Wars I & II

Farndon
- Carl's Cam Memorials: War Memorial, Farndon, Cheshire
  www.carlscam.com/warmem/farndon.htm
  World Wars I & II

Frankby
- Carl's Cam Memorials: War Memorial, Frankby, Cheshire
  www.carlscam.com/warmem/frankby.htm
  World Wars I & II; includes names from Greasby

Frodsham
- Carl's Cam Memorials: War Memorial, Frodsham, Cheshire
  www.carlscam.com/warmem/frodsham.htm
  World Wars I & II

Gatley
- Carl's Cam Memorials: War Memorial, Gatley, Cheshire
  www.carlscam.com/gatley/warmem.htm
  World Wars I & II

Gawsworth
- Carl's Cam Memorials: War Memorial, Gawsworth, Cheshire
  www.carlscam.com/gawsworth/warmem.htm
  World Wars I & II

Gee Cross
- Carl's Cam Memorials: War Memorial, Hyde Chapel, Gee Cross, Cheshire
  www.carlscam.com/geecross/chapmem.htm
  World War I

Godley
- Carl's Cam Memorials: War Memorial, St. John's Church, Godley, Cheshire
  www.carlscam.com/godley/warmem.htm
  World War I

Godley Hill
- Carl's Cam Memorials: War Memorial, Godley Hill, Cheshire
  www.carlscam.com/godley/warhill.htm
  World Wars I & II

Goostrey
- Carl's Cam Memorials: War Memorial, Goostrey, Cheshire
  www.carlscam.com/warmem/goostrey.htm
  World Wars I & II

Greasby
See Frankby

Great Barrow
- Carl's Cam Memorials: War Memorial, Great Barrow, Cheshire
  www.carlscam.com/warmem/barrow.htm
  World Wars I & II

Great Budworth
- Carl's Cam Memorials: War Memorial, Great Budworth, Cheshire
  www.carlscam.com/warmem/budworth.htm
  World Wars I & II

Great Sutton
- Carl's Cam Memorials: War Memorial, Great Sutton, Cheshire
  www.carlscam.com/warmem/gsutton.htm

Guilden Sutton
- Carl's Cam Memorials: War Memorial, Guilden Sutton, Cheshire
  www.carlscam.com/warmem/guilden.htm
  World War II

Hale
- Carl's Cam Memorials: War Memorial, Hale, Cheshire
  www.carlscam.com/warmem/hale.htm
  World Wars I & II

Hale Barns
- Carl's Cam Memorials: War Memorial, Hale Barns, Cheshire
  www.carlscam.com/warmem/halebarnsringway.htm
  World Wars I & II; includes names from Ringway

Hartford
- Carl's Cam Memorials: War Memorial, Hartford, Cheshire
  www.carlscam.com/warmem/hartford.htm
  World Wars I & II

Hatton
See Waverton

Hazel Grove
- Carl's Cam Memorials: War Memorial, Hazel Grove, Cheshire
  www.carlscam.com/hazelgrove/warmem.htm
  World Wars I & II

Heald Green
- Carl's Cam Memorials: War Memorial, Long Lane, Cheshire
  www.carlscam.com/healdgreen/longmem.htm
  In Heald Green. World Wars I & II

Heaton Mersey
- Carl's Cam Memorials: War Memorial, Heaton Mersey, Cheshire
  www.carlscam.com/heatonmersey/warmem.htm
  World Wars I & II

Heaviley
- Carl's Cam Memorials: War Memorial, Heaviley, Stockport, Cheshire
  www.carlscam.com/warmem/heaviley.htm
  World War I

Helsby
- Carl's Cam Memorials: War Memorial, Helsby, Cheshire
  www.carlscam.com/warmem/helsby.htm
  World Wars I & II

Henbury
- Carl's Cam Memorials: Henbury and Broken Cross War Memorial
  www.carlscam.com/henbury/warmem.htm
  World Wars I & II

Heswall
- Carl's Cam Memorials: War Memorial, Heswall, Cheshire
  www.carlscam.com/warmem/heswall.htm
  World Wars I & II; includes names of civilian casualties 1939-45

High Lane
- Carl's Cam Memorials: War Memorial, High Lane, Cheshire
  www.carlscam.com/highlane/warmem.htm
  World Wars I & II

Hollingworth
- Carl's Cam Memorials: War Memorial, Hollingworth, Cheshire
  www.carlscam.com/hollingworth/warmem.htm
  World Wars I & II

Holmes Chapel
- Carl's Cam Memorials: War Memorial, Holmes Chapel, Cheshire
  www.carlscam.com/warmem/hchapel.htm
  World Wars I & II

Hoole
- Carl's Cam Memorials: War Memorial, Hoole, Cheshire
  www.carlscam.com/warmem/hoole.htm
  World Wars I & II; includes names from Newton
- Hoole War Memorial
  www.users.globalnet.co.uk/~pardos/HooleMain.html

Hyde
- Carl's Cam Memorials: War Memorial, Town Hall, Hyde, Cheshire
  www.carlscam.com/hyde/warhall.htm
  World War I
- Carl's Cam Memorials: Roll of Honour, Baptist Church, Hyde, Cheshire
  www.carlscam.com/warmem/hydebap.htm
- Carl's Cam Memorials: Roll of Honour, Congregational Church, Hyde, Cheshire
  www.carlscam.com/warmem/hydecong.htm
  World War I
- Newton Wood War Memorial, Victoria Road, Hyde
  www.certificates.fsnet.co.uk/Newton%20War%20Memorial.htm
- Carl's Cam Memorials: War Memorial, Victoria Street, Newton, Hyde, Cheshire
  www.carlscam.com/newton/vicmem.htm
  World War I

- Carl's Cam Memorials: War Memorial, Newton Wood, Hyde, Cheshire
  www.carlscam.com/newton/woodmem.htm
  World Wars I & II
- Carl's Cam Memorials: Hyde, St. George's Church, Roll of Honour 1914-1919
  www.carlscam.com/warmem/hydegeo.htm

Kelsall
- Carl's Cam Memorials: War Memorial, Kelsall, Cheshire
  www.carlscam.com/kelsall.htm
  World Wars I & II, & the Korean War

Kermincham
See Swettenham

Kerridge
- Carl's Cam Memorials: War Memorial, Kerridge, Cheshire
  www.carlscam.com/kerridge/warmem.htm
  World Wars I & II

Kettleshulme
- Carl's Cam Memorials: War Memorial, Kettleshulme, Cheshire
  www.carlscam.com/kettle/warmem.htm
  World Wars I & II

Knutsford
- Carl's Cam Memorials: War Memorial, Knutsford, Cheshire
  www.carlscam.com/warmem/kford.htm
  World War I & II

Little Budworth
- Carl's Cam Memorials: War Memorials, Little Budworth, Cheshire
  www.carlscam.com/warmem/knutsford.htm
  World War I
- Carl's Cam Memorials: Roll of Honour, Little Budworth, Cheshire
  www.carlscam.com/warmem/budworth1.htm
  World War I

Lostock
- Carl's Cam Memorials: War Memorial, Lostock Works, Lostock, Cheshire
  www.carlscam.com/warmem/lostockw.htm
  World Wars I & II

Lostock Gralam
- Carl's Cam Memorials: War Memorial, Lostock Gralam, Cheshire
  www.carlscam.com/warmem/lostockg.htm
  World Wars I & II

Lostock Green
- Carl's Cam Memorials: War Memorial, Methodist Church, Lostock Green, Cheshire
  www.carlscam.com/warmem/lostockm.htm
  World Wars I & II

Lower Peover
- Carl's Cam Memorials: War Memorial, Lower Peover, Cheshire
  www.carlscam.com/warmem/peover1.htm
  World Wars I & II

Lower Walton
- Carl's Cam Memorials: War Memorial, Lower Walton, Cheshire
  www.carlscam.com/warmem/walton.htm
  World Wars I & II

Lower Whitley
- Carl's Cam Memorials: War Memorial, Lower Whitley, Cheshire
  www.carlscam.com/warmem/whitley.htm
  World War I

Lymm
- Carl's Cam Memorials: War Memorial, Lymm, Cheshire
  www.carlscam.com/lymm/warmem.htm
  World Wars I & II

Macclesfield
- Carl's Cam Memorials: War Memorial, Macclesfield, Cheshire
  www.carlscam.com/macclesfield/cheshire.htm
  World Wars I & II

Macclesfield Forest
- Carl's Cam Memorials: War Memorial Macclesfield Forest, Cheshire
  www.carlscam.com/macclesfield/forest.htm
  World War I

Malpas
- Carl's Cam Memorials: War Memorial, Malpas, Cheshire
  www.carlscam.com/warmem/malpas.htm
  World Wars I & II

Marple
- Carl's Cam Memorials: War Memorial, Marple, Cheshire
  www.carlscam.com/marple/warmem.htm
  World Wars I & II

- Carl's Cam Memorials: War Memorial, All Saints Church, Marple, Cheshire
  www.carlscam.com/marple/saints.htm
  World Wars I & II

Mere
- Carl's Cam Memorials: War Memorial, Mere, Cheshire
  www.carlscam.com/warmem/mere.htm
  World Wars I & II

Middlewich
- Carl's Cam Memorials: War Memorial, Middlewich, Cheshire
  www.carlscam.com/warmem/middlewich.htm
  World Wars I & II, and the Korean War

- Carl's Cam Memorials: War Memorial, Brunner Mond Works, Middlewich, Cheshire
  www.carlscam.com/warmem/middlewichw.htm
  World War I

Mobberley
- Carl's Cam Memorials: War Memorial, Mobberley, Cheshire
  www.carlscam.com/warmem/mobberley.htm
  World Wars I & II

Mossley
- Carl's Cam Memorials: War Memorial, Mossley, Congleton, Cheshire
  www.carlscam.com/congleton/warmem.htm
  World Wars I & II

Mottram in Longdendale
- Carl's Cam Memorials: War Memorial, Mottram in Longdendale, Cheshire
  www.carlscam.com/newton/vicmem.htm
  World Wars I & II

Moulton
- Carl's Cam Memorials: War Memorial, Moulton, Cheshire
  www.carlscam.com/warmem/moulton.htm
  World Wars I & II

Nantwich

- Carl's Cam Memorials: War Memorial, Nantwich, Cheshire
  www.carlscam.com/warmem/nantwich.htm
  World Wars I & II

Neston

- Carl's Cam Memorials: War Memorial, Neston, Cheshire
  www.carlscam.com/warmem/neston.htm
  World Wars I & II

Newton

See Hoole

Northenden

- Carl's Cam Memorials: War Memorial, Northenden, Cheshire
  www.carlscam.com/northenden/warmem.htm
  World Wars I & II

Northwich

- Carl's Cam Memorials: War Memorial, Northwich, Cheshire
  www.carlscam.com/warmem/northwich.htm
  World Wars I & II

Odd Rode

- Carl's Cam Memorials: War Memorial, Odd Rode, Cheshire
  www.carlscam.com/warmem/oddrode.htm
  World Wars I & II

Over

- Carl's Cam Memorials: War Memorial, Over, Cheshire
  www.carlscam.com/warmem/over.htm
  World Wars I & II (not yet fully transcribed)

- Carl's Cam Memorials: War Memorial, United Reformed Church, Over, Cheshire
  www.carlscam.com/warmem/overurc.htm
  World Wars I & II

Over Knutsford

- Carl's Cam Memorials: War Memorial, Over Knutsford, Cheshire
  www.carlscam.com/warmem/knutsford.htm
  World War I

Port Sunlight

- Carl's Cam Memorials: War Memorial, Port Sunlight, Cheshire
  www.carlscam.com/warmem/sunlight.htm
  World Wars I & II

Pott Shrigley

- Carl's Cam Memorials: War Memorial, Pott Shrigley, Cheshire
  www.carlscam.com/pottshrigley/warmem.htm
  World War I

Poynton

- Carl's Cam Memorials. War Memorial, Poynton, Cheshire
  www.carlscam.com/poynton/warmem.htm
  World Wars I & II

Prenton

- Carl's Cam Memorials: War Memorial, Preston, Cheshire
  www.carlscam.com/warmem/prenton.htm

Prestbury

- Carl's Cam Memorials: War Memorial, Prestbury, Cheshire
  www.carlscam.com/prestbury/warmem.htm
  World Wars I & II

Rainow

- Carl's Cam Memorials: War Memorial, Rainow, Cheshire
  www.carlscam.com/rainow/warmem.htm
  World Wars I & II

Ringway

See Hale Barns

Romiley

- Carl's Cam Memorials: War Memorial, Romiley, Cheshire
  www.carlscam.com/romiley/rommem.htm
  World War I
  See also Bredbury

Runcorn

- Carl's Cam Memorials: War Memorial, Runcorn, Cheshire
  www.carlscam.com/warmem/runcorn.htm
  World Wars I & II

Saighton

- Carl's Cam Memorials: War Memorial, Saighton, Cheshire
  www.carlscam.com/warmem/saighton.htm
  World War I

Sale

- Carl's Memorials: War Memorial, Sale, Cheshire
  www.carlscam.com/warmem/sale.htm
  World Wars I & II

- Carl's Cam Memorials: War Memorial, St. Anne, Sale, Cheshire
  www.carlscam.com/warmem/salea.htm
  World War I

Sandbach
- Carl's Cam Memorials: War Memorial, Sandbach, Cheshire
  www.carlscam.com/warmem/sandbach.htm
  World Wars I & II

- Carl's Cam Memorials: War Memorial, Sandbach Heath, Cheshire
  www.carlscam.com/warmem/sandbachh.htm
  World War I

- Carl's Cam Memorials: War Memorial, Sandbach Works, Cheshire
  www.carlscam.com/warmem/sandbachw.htm
  World War I

Saughall
- Carl's Cam Memorials: War Memorial, Saughall, Cheshire
  www.carlscam.com/warmem/saughall.htm
  World Wars I & II

Shavington
- Carl's Cam Memorials: War Memorial, Shavington, Cheshire
  www.carlscam.com/warmem/shavington.htm
  World Wars I & II

Shotwick
- Carl's Cam Memorials: War Memorial, Shotwick, Cheshire
  www.carlscam.com/warmem/shotwick.htm
  World Wars I & II

Siddington
- Carl's Cam Memorials: War Memorial, Siddington, Cheshire
  www.carlscam.com/warmem/siddington.htm
  World War I

Stalybridge
- Carl's Cam Memorials: Memorial, Stalybridge, Cheshire
  www.carlscam.com/stalybridge/warmem.htm

Stockport
- Carl's Cam Memorials: War Memorial, Stockport, Cheshire
  www.carlscam.com/stockport/warmem.htm
  World Wars I & II, and subsequently

Stockton Heath
- Carl's Cam Memorials: Memorial, Stockton Heath, Cheshire
  www.carlscam.com/warmem/stockton.htm
  World Wars I & II

Stretton
- Carl's Cam Memorials: War Memorial, Stretton, Cheshire
  www.carlscam.com/warmem/stretton.htm
  World Wars I & II

Styal
- Carl's Cam Memorials: War Memorial, Styal, Cheshire
  www.carlscam.com/styal/warmem.htm
  World Wars I & II

Sutton Lane Ends
- Carl's Cam Memorials: War Memorial, Sutton Lane Ends, Cheshire
  www.carlscam.com/sutton/warmem.htm
  World War I

Swettenham
- Carl's Cam Memorials: War Memorial, Swettenham, Cheshire
  www.carlscam.com/warmem/swettenham.htm
  World Wars I & II; includes names from Davenport and Kermincham

Tarporley
- Carl's Cam Memorials: War Memorial, Tarporley, Cheshire
  www.carlscam.com/warmem/tarporley.htm
  World Wars I & II

Tarvin
- Carl's Cam Memorials: War Memorial, Tarvin, Cheshire
  www.carlscam.com/warmem/tarvin.htm
  World Wars I & II

Tattenhall
- Carl's Cam Memorials: War Memorial, Tattenhall, Cheshire
  www.carlscam.com/warmem/tattenhall.htm
  World Wars I & II

Thelwall
- Carl's Cam Memorials: War Memorial, Thelwall, Cheshire
  www.carlscam.com/warmem/thelwall.htm
  World Wars I & II

Thornton Hough
- Carl's Cam Memorials: War Memorial, Thornton Hough, Cheshire
  www.carlscam.com/warmem/thorntonh.htm
  World War I

Thornton le Moors
- Carl's Cam Memorials: War Memorial, Thornton-le-Moors, Cheshire
  www.carlscam.com/warmem/thorntonlm.htm
  World Wars I & II

Thurstaston
- Carl's Cam Memorials: War Memorial, Thurstaston, Cheshire
  www.carlscam.com/warmem/thurstaston.htm
  World Wars I & II

Threapwood
- Carl's Cam Memorials: War Memorial, Threapwood, Cheshire
  www.carlscam.com/warmem/threapwood.htm

Tilston
- Carl's Cam Memorials: War Memorial, Tilston, Cheshire
  www.carlscam.com/warmem/tilston.htm
  World Wars I & II

Tilstone Furnell
- Carls Cam Memorials: War Memorial, St. Jude, Tilstone Furnell, Cheshire
  www.carlscam.com/warmem/tilstone.htm
  World Wars I & II

Tintwistle
- Carl's Cam Memorials: War Memorial, Tintwistle, Cheshire
  www.carlscam.com/tintwistle/memorial.htm
  World War I

Tiverton
- Carl's Cam Memorials: War Memorial, Tiverton, Cheshire
  www.carlscam.com/warmem/tiverton.htm
  World Wars I & II

Tushingham
- Carl's Cam Memorials: War Memorial, Tushingham, Cheshire
  www.carlscam.com/warmem/tushingham.htm
  World War I

Upton (near Birkenhead)
- Carl's Cam Memorials: Upton (near Birkenhead), Cheshire
  www.carlscam.com/warmem/uptonb.htm
  World Wars I & II

Upton (near Chester)
- Carl's Cam Memorials: War Memoria, Upton (near Chester), Cheshire
  www.carlscam.com/warmem/upton.htm

Utkinton
- Carl's Cam Memorials: War Memorial, Utkinton, Cheshire
  www.carlscam.com/warmem/utkinton.htm

Wallasey
- Carl's Cam Memorials: St. Hilary's, Wallasey, Cheshire
  www.carlscam.com/warmem/wallasey.htm
  World War I

- Carl's Cam Memorials: War Memorial, Wallasey, Cheshire
  www.carlscam.com/warmem/wallaseyh.htm
  World War I. In the hospital

Wallerscote
- Carl's Cam Memorials: War Memorial, Wallerscote Works, Winnington, Cheshire
  www.carlscam.com/warmem/wallerscotew.htm
  World War II

Warburton
- Carl's Cam Memorials: War Memorial, Warburton, Cheshire
  www.carlscam.com/warmem/warburton.htm
  World Wars I & II

Waverton
- Carl's Cam Memorials: War Memorial, Waverton, Cheshire
  www.carlscam.com/warmem/waverton.htm
  World Wars I & II; includes names from Hatton

Weaverham
- Carl's Cam Memorials: War Memorial, Weaverham, Cheshire
  www.carlscam.com/warmem/weaverham.htm
  World Wars I & II

West Kirby
- Carl's Cam Memorials: War Memorial, West Kirby, Cheshire
  www.carlscam.com/warmem/westkirby.htm
  World Wars I & II

Whaley Bridge
- Carl's Cam Memorials: War Memorial, Whaley Bridge, Cheshire
  www.carlscam.com/whaley/warmem.htm
  World Wars I & II

Wharton
- Carl's Cam Memorials: War Memorial, Wharton, Cheshire
  www.carlscam.com/warmem/wharton.htm
  World War I

Wheelock
- Carl's Cam Memorials: War Memorial, Wheelock, Cheshire
  www.carlscam.com/warmem/wheelock.htm
  World Wars I & II

Whitegate
- Carl's Cam Memorials: War Memorial, Whitegate, Cheshire
  www.carlscam.com/warmem/whitegate.htm
  World Wars I & II

Willaston
- Carl's Cam Memorials: War Memorial, Willaston, Cheshire
  www.carlscam.com/warmem/willaston.htm
  World Wars I & II

Wilmslow
- Carl's Cam Memorials: War Memorial, Wilmslow, Cheshire
  www.carlscam.com/wilmslow/warmem.htm
  World Wars I & II

Winnington
- Carl's Cam Memorials: War Memorial, Winnington Works, Winnington, Cheshire
  www.carlscam.com/warmem/winningtonw.htm
  World Wars I & II
  See also Wallerscote

Winsford
- Carl's Cam Memorials: War Memorial, Winsford, Cheshire
  www.carlscam.com/warmem/winsford.htm
  World Wars I & II

- Carl's Cam Memorials: Winsford Boer War Memorial, Cheshire
  www.carlscam.com/warmem/winsford.htm
  Includes list of soldiers who survived

- War Memorial, Salt Union, Winsford, Cheshire
  www.carlscam.com/warmem/winsalt.htm

Wistaston
- Carl's Cam Memorials: War Memorial, Wistaston, Cheshire
  www.carlscam.com/warmem/wistaston.htm
  World Wars I & II

- Carl's Cam Memorials: Memorial Hall, Wistaston, Cheshire
  www.carlscam.com/warmem/wistaston.htm
  World War II

Woodford
- Carl's Cam Memorials: War Memorial, Woodford, Cheshire
  www.carlscam.com/warmem/woodford.htm
  World Wars I & II

Wrenbury
- Carl's Cam Memorials: War Memorial, Wrenbury, Cheshire
  www.carlscam.com/warmem/wrenbury.htm
  World Wars I & II

- Carl's Cam Memorials: War Memorial, Wrenbury School, Cheshire
  www.carlscam.com/warmem/wrenburys.htm
  World War I

Cumberland

General
- Original Indexes ... War Memorials: Cumberland
  www.original-indexes.demon.co.uk/prices/OLB-WAR.htm
  List of transcripts for sale

Penrith
- Penrith War Memorials
  www.zeonlair.demon.co.uk/famtree/war.htm

Derbyshire

General
- Chesterfield Sherwoods on the Somme
  www.multeen.freeserve.co.uk/Village%20Memorials%20A-D.htm
  Collection of photographs of Derbyshire village memorials, some
  individually listed below. Continued at
  /Village%20Memorials%20E-M.htm and
  /Village%20Memorials%20N-7.htm

Alfreton
- [Alfreton War Memorial]
  www.multeen.freeserve.co.uk/images/Alfreton%20201.jpg

Ashbourne
- [Ashbourne Memorial Plaque]
  www.multeen.freeserve.co.uk/images/
  Ashbourne%20names%20-%20officers%20and%20OR.jpg

Ashford
- [Ashford in the Water War Memorial]
  www.multeen.freeserve.co.uk/images/Ashford%20Names.jpg
  World War I

Ashover
- World Wars I & II: Ashover casualties
  familytreemaker.genealogy.com/users/m/i/l/John-Mills/FILE/0001page.html

- Ashover War Memorial
  www.fv76.dial.pipex.com/warmem.htm
  World Wars I & II

Bonsall
- [Bonsall Village Memorial]
  www.multeen.freeserve.co.uk/images/Bonsall%201.jpg
  World War I

Brassington
- Brassington War Memorial
  www.brassington.org/warmem.htm

Brimington
- Brimington War Memorial 1914-1918
  www.skimber.demon.co.uk/brim/warm.htm

Burbage
- [Burbage War Memorial]
www.multeen.freeserve.co.uk/images/BURBAGE%202.jpg
World War I

Calver
- [Calver War Memorial]
www.multeen.freeserve.co.uk/images/Calver%20memorial2.jpg

Charlesworth
- Carl's Cam Memorials: War Memorial, Charlesworth, Derbyshire
www.carlscam.com/charlesworth/warmem.htm

Chesterfield
- Old Cestrefeldians in the Great War
www.multeen.freeserve.co.uk/
Old020Cestrefeldians%20War%20War%20Memorial.htm

Cromford
- Cromford Village in Derbyshire: the History Zone
www.pandyweb.freeserve.co.uk/crom__his.html
Includes war memorials, World Wars I & II

Eckington
- Holy Trinity, Eckington
med441.bham.ac.uk/eckington.html
War memorials

Froggatt
- [Froggatt War Memorial]
www.multeen.freeserve.co.uk/images/froggatt.jpg

Furness Vale
- Carl's Cam Memorials: War Memorial, Furness Vale, Derbyshire
www.carlscam.com/whaley/furness.htm
World Wars I & II

Glossop
Carl's Cam Memorials: War Memorial, Glossop, Derbyshire
www.carlscam.com/warmem/glossop.htm
World Wars I & II

Grassmoor
- Grassmoor War Memorial: World War I
familytreemaker.genealogy.com/users/m/i/l/John-Mills/FILE/0008page.html

Grindleford
- War Memorial: Grindleford, Derbyshire
www.genuki.org.uk/big/eng/DBY/Grindleford/WarMem.html

Gurbar
- [Gurbar War memorial]
www.multeen.freeserve.co.uk/images/curbar.jpg

Hadfield
- Carl's Cam Memorials: War Memorial, Hadfield, Derbyshire
www.carlscam.com/warmem/hadfield.htm
World Wars I & II

Hasland
- [Hasland Village War Memorial]
www.multeen.freeserve.co.uk/images/Hasland%20A-F.jpg
Continued at /Hasland%20G-M.jpg and /Hasland%20K-W.jpg

Hope
- Inhabitants of the Parish of Hope who served overseas in the Great European War 1914-1918
www.genuki.org.uk/big/eng/DBY/Hope/Notes/ChapterXII.html

Langley Mill
- War Memorial, Langley Mill, Derbyshire
www.boer-war-medals.co.uk/langley.html
Boer War memorial

Matlock
- Matlock and Matlock Bath, Derbyshire: the War Memorials
www.andrewspages.dial.pipex.com/matlock/warmem.htm

Mellor
- Carl's Cam Memorials: War Memorial, Mellor, Derbyshire
www.carlscam.com/mellor/warmem.htm
World Wars I & II, and the Korean War

Morton
- Morton Village Memorial
www.multeen.freeserve.co.uk/images/Morton%202.jpg
World War I

Newbold
- [Newbold War memorial]
www.multeen.freeserve.co.uk/images/Newbold.jpg
World War I

North Wingfield
- North Wingfield War Memorial: World War I
  familytreemaker.genealogy.com/mi/i/l/John-Mills/FILE/0015page.html

Old Brampton
- [Old Brampton War memorial]
  www.multeen.freeserve.co.uk/images/Old%20Brampton%202.jpg
  World War I

Parwich
- Parwich War Memorial
  www.parwichchurch.co.uk/warmemorial.htm

Peak Dale
- Peak Dale War Memorial
  www.multeen.freeserve.co.uk/images/Peak%20Dale%205.jpg
  Continued at:
      /Peak%20Dale%204.jpg
      /Peak%20Dale%201.jpg
      /Peak%20Dale%202.jpg
      /Peak%20Dale%203.jpg

Pilsley
- [Pilsley War Memorial 1914-18]
  www.multeen.freeserve.co.uk/images/Pilsley%203.jpg

Stanley
- Stanley War Memorial
  freepages.genealogy.rootsweb.com/~alanbloor/WarMemorial.htm
  World Wars I & II

- Roll of Honour, 1914-1919
  freepages.genealogy.rootsweb.com/~alanbloor/RollofHonour.htm
  For Stanley

Staveley
- In Grateful Remembrance of the Men of the parish (Staveley) who fell in
  the War at 1914-1919
  www.multeen.freeserve.co.uk/images/stav%202a.jpg

Stonebroom
- [Stonebroom War Memorial 1914-18]
  www.multeen.freeserve.co.uk/images/Stonebroom%202.jpg

Stoney Middleton
- [Stoney Middleton War Memorial]
  www.multeen.freeserve.co.uk/images/S%20Middleton%20A-Z.jpg

- War Memorial, Stoney Middleton, Derbyshire
  www.genuki.org.uk/big/eng/DBY/StoneyMiddleton/WarMem.html

Tansley
- Tansley Village: men from Tansley who died in Word War I
  freespace.virgin.net/pat.gaskell/warmem1.html

Tibshelf
- Tibshelf: men who died in the Great War 1914-1918
  www.genealogy-links.co.uk/html/tibshelf.men.html

- The Tibshelf War Memorial 1914-1919
  www.hesketha.freeserve.co.uk/wwi/memorials/tibshelfwarmem.htm

- [Tibshelf War Memorial]
  www.multeen.freeserve.co.uk/images/Tib%20WarMem1.jpg
  Continued at
      /Tib%20MemAtoC.jpg
      /Tib%20MemCtoS.jpg
      /Tib%20MemStoW.jpg

Wadshelf
- [Wadshelf War Memorial]
  www.multeen.freeserve.co.uk/images/wadshelf.jpg

Whittington
- Bushes Memorial, Whittington, Chesterfield
  www.multeen.freeserve.co.uk/images/Bushes%20-%20names.jpg
  World War I

Durham

Barnard Castle
- War Memorial: Barnard Castle St. Mary, Co. Durham
  www.original-indexes.demon.co.uk/DUR/BAR/WMBARBAR.htm

Boldon
- War Memorial: Boldon, Co. Durham
  www.original-indexes.demon.co.uk/DUR/JAR/WMJARBOL.htm
  World War I and II

Bournmoor
- War Memorial: Bournmoor St. Barnabus, Co. Durham
  www.original-indexes.demon.co.uk/DUR/HSP/WMHSPBOU.htm

Byers Green
- War Memorial: Byers Green, Co. Durham
  www.original-indexes.demon.co.uk/DUR/AUC/WMAUCBYE.htm

Chopwell
- War Memorial: Chopwell, Co. Durham
  www.original-indexes.demon.co.uk/DUR/GAW/WMGAWCHO.htm

Cockfield
- War Memorial: Cockfield, Co. Durham
  www.original-indexes.demon.co.uk/DUR/BAR/WMBARCOC.htm

Crook
- War Memorial: Crook, Co. Durham
  www.original-indexes.demon.co.uk/DUR/STP/WMSTPCSC.htm
  World War I, II and Korean War

Darlington
- Unveiling of Bradford Memorial Plaque and Rededication of War
  Memorial Window: Darlington Queen Elizabeth Sixth Form College
  www.geocities.com/bradcrem/bradford__memorial.html

- War Memorial: Darlington, Co. Durham
  www.original-indexes.demon.co.uk/DUR/DAR/WMDARDAR.htm
  Boer War, 1899-1902

Dunston
- Dunston Roll of Honour: the names of men who gave their lives in the
  Great War 1914-1918
  www.genuki.org.uk/big/eng/DUR/GatesheadWarDead/Dunston.html

Durham
- War Memorial: Durham County Hall, Co. Durham
  www.original-indexes.demon.co.uk/DUR/DUR/WMDURDUR.htm

Ebchester
- War Memorial: Ebchester St Ebba, Co Durham
  www.original-indexes.demon.co.uk/DUR/LAN/WMLANEBC.htm
  World Wars I and II

Edmundbyers
- War Memorial: Edmundbyers St. Edmund, Co. Durham
  www.original-indexes.co.uk/DUR/STP/WMSTPEDM.htm

Frosterley
- War Memorial: Frosterley, Co. Durham
  www.original-indexes.demon.co.uk/DUR/STP/WMSTPFSM.htm

Gateshead
- Gateshead East Cemetery. Cemetery Register: WWI Servicemen
  www.genuki.org.uk/big/eng/DUR/GatesheadWarDead/East1.htm

- Gateshead County Borough War Dead 1914-1918
  www.genuki.org.uk/big/eng/DUR/GatesheadWarDead/

- Names from the WWI Memorial at St. James Church, Gateshead
  www.genuki.org.uk/big/eng/DUR/StJamesMem.html

- Names on the Boer War Memorials at Durham Road, Low Fell, and
  Saltwell Park, Gateshead
  www.genuki.org.uk/big/eng/DUR/GatesheadWarDead/BoerMemorial.html

Greenside
- War Memorial: Greenside, Co. Durham
  www.original-indexes.demon.co.uk/DUR/GAW/WMGAWGSJ.htm

Hartlepool
- War Memorials in Hartlepool
  www.contango.demon.co.uk/warmem.html

- South Durham Steel & Iron Co. War Memorial, Hartlepool
  www.contango.demon.co.uk/southdurham.html

Helmington Row
- War Memorial: Helmington Row, Co. Durham
  www.original-indexes.demon.co.uk/DUR/STP/WMSTPHEL.htm

High Spen
- War Memorial: High Spen St. Patrick
  www.original-indexes.demon.co.uk/DUR/GAW/WMGAWSSP.htm

- Names from the War Memorial and Military Graves at High Spen,
  St. Patrick
  www.swinhope.demon.co.uk/genuki/Transcriptions/HSN-RoH.html

Houghton le Spring
- War Memorial: Houghton-le-Spring & All Angels, Co. Durham
  www.original-indexes.demon.co.uk/DUR/HSP/WMHSPHSP.htm

Hunwick
- War Memorial: Hunwick St. Paul
  www.original-indexes.demon.co.uk/DUR/AUC/WMAUCHUN.html

Lumley
- War Memorial: Lumley Christ Church
  www.original-indexes.demon.co.uk/DUR/CLS/WMCLSLCC.htm

Marley Hill
- Marley Hill and District Roll of Honour: the names of men who gave
  their lives in the Great War 1914-1918
  www.genuki.org.uk/big/eng/DUR/GatesdeadWarDead/MarleyHill.html

Muggleswick
- War Memorial: Muggleswick All Saints, Co. Durham
  www.original-indexes.demon.co.uk/DUR/STP/WMSTPMUG.htm

Newfield
- War Memorial: Newfield, Co. Durham
  www.original-indexes.demon.co.uk/DUR/AUC/WMAUCNEW.htm

Norton
- [Norton]: War Memorial Search Results Page
  www.war-memorials.org.uk/
  click on 'Durham' and 'Norton'

Penshaw
- War Memorial: Penshaw, Co. Durham
  www.original-indexes.demon.co.uk/DUR/HSP/WMHSPPEN.htm
  World War I

Redmarshall
- War Memorial: Redmarshall St. Cuthbert, Co. Durham
  www.original-indexes.demon.co.uk/DUR/STO/WMSTORED.htm

Rookhope
- War Memorial: Rookhope St. John, Co. Durham
  www.original-indexes.demon.co.uk/DUR/STP/WMSTPRSJ.htm

Rowlands Gill
- Rowlands Gill Casualties of the World Wars
  www.swinhope.demon.co.uk/genuki/Transcriptions/RGL-RoH.html

- Rowlands Gill Roll of Honour: the names, ranks and regiments of men
  who gave their lives in the Great War 1914-1918
  www.genuki.org.uk/big/eng/DUR/GatesheadWarDead/RGill.html

Sacriston
- War Memorial: Sacriston, Co. Durham
  www.original-indexes.demon.co.uk/DUR/DUR/WMDURSAC.htm

St. Johns Chapel
- War Memorial: St. Johns Chapel, Co. Durham
  www.original-indexes.demon.co.uk/DUR/STP/WMSTPSJC.htm

Shadforth
- War Memorial: Shadforth, Co. Durham
  www.original-indexes.demon.co.uk/DUR/DUR/WMDURSHA.htm
  World War I

Shildon
- Shildon War Memorial 1939-1955
  www.ish-s.org.uk/warmem.htm

South Shields
- W.W.I. Roll of Honour
  members.tripod.com/geordie_gen/ww1roll.htm
  For South Shields

- St. Stephens Church, Mile End Road, South Shields 1914-1918 Memorial
  members.tripod.com/geordie_gen/stephmem.htm

Staindrop
- War Memorial: Staindrop St. Mary, Co. Durham
  www.original-indexes.demon.co.uk/DUR/BAR/WMBARSTD.htm

Stanhope

- War Memorial: Stanhope St. Thomas
  www.original-indexes.demon.co.uk/DUR/STP/WMSTPSTP.htm

Sunderland

- War Memorial: Sunderland Post Office
  www.original-indexes.demon.co.uk/DUR/WEA/WMWEASUN.htm

Swalwell

- Swalwell Roll of Honour: the names of men who gave their lives in the
  Great War 1914-1918
  www.genuki.org.uk/big/eng/DUR/GatesheadWarDead/Swalwell.html

Teesside

- [Sir William Turner's Grammar School, Teesside:] War Memorials Search
  Results Page
  www.war-memorials.org.uk/
  Click on 'Teeside' and title

Tow Law

- Original Indexes Research Notes: War Memorial: Tow Law Sts.
  Philip & James, Co. Durham
  www.original-indexes.co.uk/DUR/STP/WMSTPTLP.htm

West Rainton

- War Memorial: West Rainton St. Mary, Co. Durham
  www.original-indexes.demon.co.uk/DUR/HSP/WMHSPWRA.htm

- West Rainton Rolls of Honour
  www.swinhope.demon.co.uk/genuki/Transcriptions/WRA-RoH.html

Westgate

- War Memorial: Westgate, Co. Durham
  www.original-indexes.demon.co.uk/DUR/STP/WMSTPSTP.htm

Whickham

- Whickham Roll of Honour: the names of men who gave their lives in
  the Great War 1914-1918
  www.genuki.org.uk/big/eng/DUR/GatesheadWarDead/Whickham.html

Whitburn

- War Memorial: Whitburn, Co. Durham
  www.original-indexes.demon.co.uk/DUR/WEA/WMWEAWBN.htm

Willington

- War Memorial: Willington St. Stephen, Co. Durham
  www.original-indexes.demon.co.uk/DUR/AVC/WMAUCWIL.htm

Winlaton

- War Memorial: Winlaton, St. Paul, Co. Durham
  www.original-indexes.demon.co.uk/DUR/GAW/WMGAWWIN.htm

Witton Gilbert

- War Memorial: Witton Gilbert, Co. Durham
  www.original-indexes.demon.co.uk/DUR/DUR/WMDURWIT.htm

Wolsingham

- Originaly Indexes Research Notes: War Memorial, Wolsingham Sts.
  Mary & Stephen, Co. Durham
  www.original-indexes.co.uk/DUR/STP/WMSTPWOL.htm

Wolviston

- War Memorial: Wolviston, Co. Durham
  www.original-indexes.demon.co.uk/DUR/STO/WMSTOWOV.htm

- [Wolviston]: War Memorials Search Results Page
  www.war-memorials.org.uk/
  Click on 'Durham' and 'Wolviston'.

Essex

General
- Register of Essex related Dead of World War II
  www.goring1941.freeserve.co.uk/reg01.html
  In progress

- Essex Police Memorial Trust
  www.essex.police.uk/memorial
  Memorial to staff killed on duty, including war deaths

- South East Essex War Memorials and Monumental Inscriptions Project
  www.goring1941.freeserve.co.uk/seewmami.html
  Lists transcripts available

Abberton
- Roll of Honour
  www.geocities.com/abbertonroh/
  Abberton & Langenhoe

Berechurch
- War Memorial
  www.stmargcol.org.uk/war.htm
  For Berechurch, World War I

Colchester
- Colchester Heroes
  www.camulos.com/war/
  War memorials

- The Christ Church War Memorial in Colchester
  www.camulos.com/war/christ.htm

- The Lexden Colchester War Memorial Index
  www.camulos.com/war/lexden1.htm

- Memorial Inscriptions at the Mile End, Colchester War Memorial
  www.camulos.com/mileend.htm

- Shrub End, Colchester, War Memorial Inscriptions
  www.camulos.com/war/shrubend.htm

Colne Engaine
- Colne Engaine War Memorial at St. Andrews Church
  www.colnevalley.demon.co.uk/Wardead.htm
  World Wars I & II

Finchingfield
- Finchingfield W.W.I. & W.W.II. Memorial
  www.essexvillages.net/essex/finchingfield/indexes/
  finchingfieldmemorial.html

Great Bentley
- Great Bentley War Memorial
  www.greatbentley.info/WarMemorial.htm
  World Wars I & II

Great Chishill
- Great Chishill (Essex) Roll of Honour
  www.roll-of-honour.com/OtherCounties/GreatChishill.html
  World War I

Hempstead
- Hempstead W.W.I. Memorial
  www.essexvillages.net/essex/hempstead/indexes/
  hempsteadmemorial.html

Heydon
- Heydon (Essex) War Memorial: Roll of Honour
  www.roll-of-honour.com/OtherCounties/Heydon.html
  World Wars I & II

Kelvedon Hatch
- Kelvedon Hatch, Essex: Local and Family History: War Memorial
  www.historyhouse.co.uk/memorial.html

Langenhoe
See Abberton

Little Hallingbury
- Little Hallingbury War Memorial
  www.anvil.clara.net/wmem.htm

Romford
- Romford Now and Then
  www.romford.org/
  Click on 'Wartime' for memorials (including the Boer War)

Silvertown
- Carl's Cam War Memorials: Silvertown Works War Memorial
  www.carlscam.com/warmem/silvertownw.htm
  World Wars I & II

Southend
- St. Erkenwalds, Southchurch Avenue, Southend on Sea: the War Memorial
  www.st-erkenwalds.co.uk/the_war_memorial.htm
  World War I

Steeple Bumpstead
- Steeple Bumpstead WWI & WWII Memorial
  www.essexvillages.net/essex/steeplebumpstead/indexes/ sbumpsteadmemorial.html

Takely
- Takely W.W.I. & W.W.II. Memorial
  www.essexvillages.net/essex/takely/indexes/takelymemorial.html

Hertfordshire

General
- Local Graves and Memorials
  www.stephen-stratford.co.uk/local_graves.htm
  Collection of war memorial pages, mainly Hertfordshire

Abbeydore
- Remembering the Great War: St. Mary's Church, Abbeydore, Hertfordshire
  www.hellfire-corner.demon.co.uk/Westlake8.htm

Apsley End
- Apsley End
  www.stephen-stratford.co.uk/apsley_end.htm

Baldock
- The War Memorial, Baldock
  www.andy.mabbett.care4free.net/baldock/

Berkhamstead
- Berkhamstead War Memorial
  www.stephen-stratford.co.uk/berkhamstead.htm
  World Wars I & II

Hemel Hempstead
- Hemel Hempstead
  www.stephen-stratford.co.uk/hemel_hempstead.htm
  World Wars I & II, and later conflicts

Hertford
- Hertford War Memorial
  www.hertfordtown.fsnet.co.uk/home.htm

Hexton
- Hexton (Herts) War Memorial
  www.roll-of-honour.com/OtherCounties/HextonRollofHonour.html
  World Wars I & II

Hinxworth
- Hinxworth (Herts) War Memorial
  www.roll-of-honour.com/OtherCounties/HinxworthRollofHonour.html
  World Wars I & II

Leverstock Green
- Leverstock Green
  www.stephen-stratford.co.uk/lg_memorial.htm
  World Wars I & II

Lilley
- Lilley (Herts) War Memorial
  www.roll-of-honour.com/OtherCounties/LilleyRollofHonour.html
  World Wars I & II

Markyate
- Markyate War Memorial
  www.roll-of-honour.com/OtherCounties/Markyate.html
  World Wars I & II

North Mimms
- North Mymms War Memorial
  www.brookmans.com/history/memorial/memorialalley.shtml
  World Wars I & II

Odsey
- Odsey, Hertfordshire Roll of Honour
  www.roll-of-honour.com/OtherCounties/Odsey.html
  World Wars I & II

Offley
- Offley, Hertfordshire Roll of Honour
  www.roll-of-honour.com/OtherCounties/OffleyRollofHonour.html
  World Wars I & II

St. Albans
- St. Albans War Memorial
  www.stephen-stratford.co.uk/stalbans.htm
  World Wars I & II

- St. Albans Abbey, Herts: Roll of Honour
  www.roll-of-honour.com/OtherCounties/StAlbansAbbeyRollofHonour.html
  World War I

Tring
- Tring War Memorial
  www.stephen-stratford.co.uk/tring.htm
  World Wars I & II

Willian
- Willian (Herts) Roll of Honour
  www.roll-of-honour.com/OtherCounties/WillianRollofHonour.com
  World War I

Huntingdonshire

General
See also Cambridgeshire

- Local War Memorials
  www.huntscycles.co.uk/Local%20Memorials.htm
  Many pages (individually listed below) of memorials to men of the Huntingdonshire Cyclist Battalions

- Roll of Honour: Huntingdonshire
  www.roll-of-honour.com/Huntingdonshire/
  Collection of web pages separately listed below

- Huntingdonshire Boer War Memorial
  www.roll-of-honour.com/Huntingdonshire/HuntingdonshireBoer.html

- Others: Roll of Honour
  www.roll-of-honour.com/Huntingdonshire/HuntsOthers.html
  World World I Airmen & Soldiers

Abbotsley
- Abbotsley War Memorial
  www.huntscycles.co.uk/Memorials/Abbotsley.htm
  World War I

- Abbotsley: Roll of Honour
  www.roll-of-honour.com/Huntingdonshire/Abbotsley.html
  World Wars I & II

Alconbury
- Alconbury Ss. Peter & Paul: Roll of Honour
  www.roll-of-honour.com/Huntingdonshire/AlconburySSPeterPaul.html
  World Wars I & II

Bluntisham
- Bluntisham War Memorial
  www.huntscycles.co.uk/Memorials/Bluntisham.htm

- Bluntisham-Cum-Earith: Roll of Honour
  www.roll-of-honour.com/Huntingdonshire/BluntishamandEarith.html
  World Wars I & II

Brampton
- Brampton War Memorial
  www.roll-of-honour.com/Huntingdonshire/Brampton.html
  World Wars I & II

Broughton
- Broughton War Memorial
  www.huntscycles.co.uk/Memorials/Broughton.htm
  World War I

- Broughton Roll of Honour
  www.roll-of-honour.com/Huntingdonshire/Broughton.html
  World Wars I & II

Buckden
- Buckden War Memorial
  www.huntscycles.co.uk/Memorials/Buckden.htm
  World War I

- Buckden Roll of Honour
  www.roll-of-honour.com/Huntingdonshire/Buckden.html
  World Wars I & II

- Buckden Baptist Roll of Honour
  www.roll-of-honour.com/Huntingdonshire/BuckdenBaptist.html
  World War I

Bury
- Bury Roll of Honour
  www.roll-of-honour.com/Huntingdonshire/Bury.html
  World War I

Colne
- Colne War Memorial
  www.huntscycles.co.uk/Memorials/Colne.htm

- Colne Roll of Honour
  www.roll-of-honour.com/Huntingdonshire/Colne.html
  World Wars I & II

Conington

- Conington War Memorial: Roll of Honour
  www.roll-of-honour.com/Huntingdonshire/Conington.html
  World War I

Covington

- Covington Roll of Honour
  www.roll-of-honour.com/Huntingdonshire/Covington.html
  World War I

Diddington

- Diddington War Memorial
  www.huntscycles.co.uk/Memorials/Diddington.htm
  World Wars I & II

- Diddington Roll of Honour
  www.roll-of-honour.com/Huntingdonshire/DiddingtonRollofHonour.htm
  World War I

Earith
See Bluntisham

Easton

- Easton Roll of Honour
  www.roll-of-honour.com/Huntingdonshire/Easton.html
  World War I

Ellington

- Ellington Roll of Honour
  www.roll-of-honour.com/Huntingdonshire/Ellington.html
  World War I

Elton

- Elton Roll of Honour
  www.roll-of-honour.com/Huntingdonshire/Elton.html
  World War I

Eynesbury

- Eynesbury War Memorial
  www.huntscycles.co.uk/Memorials/Eynesbury.htm
  World War I

- Eynesbury Roll of Honour
  www.roll-of-honour.com/Huntingdonshire/Eynesbury.html
  World Wars I & II

Fenstanton

- Fenstanton War Memorial
  www.huntscycles.co.uk/Memorials/Fenstanton.htm
  World War I

- Fenstanton Roll of Honour
  www.roll-of-honour.com/Huntingdonshire/Fenstanton.html
  World Wars I & II

Fenton
See Pidley

Godmanchester

- Godmanchester War Memorial
  www.huntscycles.co.uk/Memorials/Godmanchester.htm
  World War I

- Godmanchester War Memorial
  www.roll-of-honour.com/Huntingdonshire/Godmanchester.html
  World Wars I & II

Great Catworth

- Great Catworth Roll of Honour
  www.roll-of-honour.com/Huntingdonshire/GreatCatworth.html
  World Wars I & II

Great Gidding

- Great Gidding St. Michael Roll of Honour
  www.roll-of-honour.com/Huntingdonshire/GreatGiddingStMichael.html
  World War I

Great Gransden

- Great Gransden Roll of Honour
  www.roll-of-honour.com/Huntingdonshire/GreatGransden.html
  World Wars I & II

- Great Gransden Canadian Airforce War Memorial
  www.roll-of-honour.com/Huntingdonshire/GreatGransdenCanadian.html
  World War I

Great Paxton

- Gt. Paxton War Memorial
  www.huntscycles.co.uk/Memorials/Gt%20Paxton.htm

- Great Paxton Roll of Honour
  www.roll-of-honour.com/Huntingdonshire/GreatPaxton.html
  World Wars I & II

Great Stukeley

- Gt. Stukeley War Memorial
  www.huntscycles.co.uk/Memorials/Gt%20Stukeley.htm
  World War I

Hail Weston

- Hail Weston Roll of Honour
  www.roll-of-honour.com/Huntingdonshire/HailWeston.html
  World War I

Hemingford

- Hemingford War Scroll
  www.huntscycles.co.uk/Memorials/Hemingford.htm
  World War I

Hemingford Abbots

- Hemingford Abbots Roll of Honour
  www.roll-of-honour.com/Huntingdonshire/HemingfordAbbots.html
  World War I

Hemingford Grey

- Hemingford Grey Roll of Honour WWI
  www.roll-of-honour.com/Huntingdonshire/HemingfordGray.html
  World Wars I & II

Hilton

- Hilton War Memorial
  www.roll-of-honour.com/Huntingdonshire/Hilton.html
  World War I with detailed information

Holme

- Holme: Roll of Honour
  www.roll-of-honour.com/Huntingdonshire/Holme.html
  World Wars I & II

Holywell

- Holywell cum Needingworth War Memorial
  www.huntscycles.co.uk/Memorials/
  Holywell%20Cum%20Needingworth.htm
  World Wars I & II

- Holywell-cum-Needingworth Roll of Honour
  www.roll-of-honour.com/Huntingdonshire/HolywellcumNeedingworth.html
  World Wars I & II

Houghton

- Houghton with Wyton Roll of Honour
  www.roll-of-honour.com/Huntingdonshire/Houghton.html
  World Wars I & II

- Houghton & Wyton War Memorial
  www.huntscycles.co.uk/Memorials/Wyton.htm
  World War I

Huntingdon

- Huntingdon War Memorial
  www.huntscycles.co.uk/Memorials/Huntingdon.htm

- Huntingdon War Memorial
  www.roll-of-honour.com/Huntingdonshire/Huntingdon.html
  World War I

Kimbolton

- Kimbolton Roll of Honour
  www.roll-of-honour.com/Huntingdonshire/Kimbolton.html
  World Wars I & II

- Kimbolton War Memorial
  www.huntscycles.co.uk/Memorials/Kimbolton.htm
  World War I

Kings Ripton

- Kings Ripton Roll of Honour
  www.roll-of-honour.com/Huntingdonshire/KingsRipton.html
  World War I

- Kings Ripton War Memorial
  www.huntscycles.co.uk/Memorials/Kings%20Ripton.htm
  World War I

Leighton Bromswold

- Leighton Bromswold Roll of Honour
  www.roll-of-honour.com/Huntingdonshire/LeightonBromswold.html
  World War I

- Leighton Bromswold War Memorial
  www.huntscycles.co.uk/Memorials/Leighton%20Bromswold.htm
  Forthcoming

Little Paxton

- Little Paxton Roll of Honour
  www.roll-of-honour.com/Huntingdonshire/LittlePaxton.html
  World War I

Little Stukeley

- Little Stukeley War Memorial
  www.huntscycles.co.uk/Memorials/Little%20Stukeley.htm
  World War I

Lutton

- Lutton: Roll of Honour
  www.roll-of-honour.com/Huntingdonshire/Lutton.html
  World War I

Molesworth

- Molesworth Roll of Honour
  www.roll-of-honour.com/Huntingdonshire/Molesworth.html
  World War I

Moreborne

- Moreborne: Roll of Honour
  www.roll-of-honour.com/Huntingdonshire/Morborne.html

Needingworth

  See Holywell

Norman Cross

- Norman Cross Napoleonic Memorial: Roll of Honour
  www.roll-of-honour.com/Huntingdonshire/NormanCrossEagle.html

Offord Cluny

- Offord Cluny Roll of Honour
  www.roll-of-honour.com/Huntingdonshire/OffordCluny.html
  World Wars I & II

- Offord Cluny War Memorial
  www.huntscycles.co.uk/Memorials/Offord%20Cluny.htm
  World Wars I & II

Old Weston

- Old Weston: Roll of Honour
  www.roll-of-honour.com/Huntingdonshire/OldWeston.html
  World Wars I & II

Pidley

- Pidley War Memorial
  www.huntscycles.co.uk/Memorials/Pidley.htm
  World Wars I & II

- Pidley-cum-Fenton: Roll of Honour
  www.roll-of-honour.com/Huntingdonshire/PidleycumFenton.html

Pondersbridge

- Pondersbridge: Roll of Honour
  www.roll-of-honour.com/Huntingdonshire/Pondersbridge.html
  World War I

Ramsey

- Ramsey War Memorial
  www.huntscycles.co.uk/Memorials/Ramsey.htm
  Forthcoming

- Ramsey War Memorial
  www.roll-of-honour.com/Huntingdonshire/Ramsey.html
  World Wars I & II

- Ramsey St. Mary's War Memorial
  www.huntscycles.co.uk/Memorials/Ramsey%20St%20Marys.htm
  World War I

St. Ives

- St. Ives: Roll of Honour
  www.roll-of-honour.com/Huntingdonshire/StIves.html
  World War I

- St. Ives War Memorial
  www.huntscycles.co.uk/Memorials/St%20Ives.htm
  World War I

- War Memorial Inscriptions in St. Ives
  www.stives-tc.org.uk/public/cemeteries/war__memorial.htm
  World Wars I & II

St. Neots

- St. Neots: Roll of Honour
  www.roll-of-honour.com/Huntingdonshire/StNeots.html
  World Wars I & II

- St. Neots War Memorial
  www.huntscycles.co.uk/Memorials/St%20Neots.htm

Sawtry

- Sawtry: Roll of Honour
  www.roll-of-honour.com/Huntingdonshire/Sawtry.html
  World Wars I & II

Somersham

- Somersham: Roll of Honour
  www.roll-of-honour.com/Huntingdonshire/Somersham.html
  World Wars I & II

- Somersham War Memorial
  www.huntscycles.co.uk/Memorials/Somersham.htm
  World War I

Spaldwick

- Spaldwick: Roll of Honour
  www.roll-of-honour.com/Huntingdonshire/Spaldwick.html
  World Wars I & II, & Korean War

- Spaldwick War Memorial
  www.huntscycles.co.uk/Memorials/Spaldwick.htm
  World War I

Steeple Gidding

- Steeple Gidding-Victory Bible: Roll of Honour
  www.roll-of-honour.com/Huntingdonshire/SteepleGiddingVictoryBible.html
  World War I

Stilton

- Stilton: Memorial Hall
  www.roll-of-honour.com/Huntingdonshire/Stilton.html
  Roll of honour, World Wars I & II

- Stilton War Memorial
  www.huntscycles.co.uk/Memorials/Stilton.htm
  World War I

Stow Longa

- Stow Longa War Memorial
  www.huntscycles.co.uk/Memorials/Stow%20Longa.htm
  Forthcoming

Tilbrook

- Tilbrook: Roll of Honour
  www.roll-of-honour.com/Huntingdonshire/Tilbrook.html
  World War I

Toseland

- Toseland: Roll of Honour
  www.roll-of-honour.com/Huntingdonshire/Toseland.html
  World Wars I & II

Upwood

- Upwood War Memorial
  www.huntscycles.co.uk/Memorials/Upwood.htm
  Forthcoming

Warboys

- Warboys: Roll of Honour
  www.roll-of-honour.com/Huntingdonshire/Warboys.html
  World Wars I & II

- Warboys War Memorial
  www.huntscycles.co.uk/Memorials/Warboys.htm
  World Wars I & II

Wood Walton

- Woodwalton War Memorial
  www.huntscycles.co.uk/Memorials/Woodwalton.htm
  World War I

Wyton
See Houghton

Yaxley
- Yaxley War Memorial
  www.huntscycles.co.uk/Memorials/Yaxley.htm
  World War I

Lancashire

General
- [War Memorials of the Tameside Area]
  www.certificates.fsnet.co.uk/war%20memorial.htm
  Collection of memorial pages, also listed here separately by place

Accrington
- Greater Accrington Roll of Honour 1914-1919
  www.btinternet.com/~a.jackson/honour.htm

- The Accrington Pals
  www.btinternet.com/~a.jackson/pals__e.htm
  Includes list of officers and men

Altham
- Altham Roll of Honour 1914-1919
  www.btinternet.com/~a.jackson/altham.htm

Ashton under Lyme
- The Names of those who gave their lives for King and Country during
  the Great War of 1914 to 1919 from the town of Ashton under Lyme
  www.certificates.fsnet.co.uk/war20memorial.htm
  Click on 'Ashton under Lyme Memorial'

Baxenden
- Baxenden Roll of Honour 1914-1919
  www.btinternet.com/~a.jackson/baxenden.htm

Bradshaw
- To the glory of God in the memory of the men of Bradshaw who died
  for their country in the Great War 1914 to 1918.
  www.certificates.fsnet.co.uk/Bradshaw%20War%20Memorial.htm
  World Wars I & II

Cartmel
- Cartmel War Memorials and Priory Church
  homepage.ntlworld.com/howard.martin/

Church
- Church Roll of Honour 1914-1919
  www.btinternet.com/~a.jackson/Church.htm

Clayton
- Manchester, Clayton / St. Cross War Memorial
  www.billnkaz.devon.co.uk/clayton.htm
  World Wars I & II, *etc.*

Clayton le Moors
- Clayton-le-Moors Roll of Honour 1914-1919
  www.btinternet.com/~a.jackson/clayton__ah.htm
  Continued at **/clayton__iz.htm**

Denton
- Carl's Cam Memorials: War Memorial, Denton, Lancashire
  www.carlscam.com/denton/warmem.htm
  World War I

Droylsden
- Droylsden Boer War Memorial
  www.billnkaz.demon.co.uk/boerwar.htm

- Droylsden Roll of Honour 1914-1918
  www.billnkaz.demon.co.uk/droymem.htm
  Continued at **/droymem3.htm**

- Droylsden Roll of Honour 1939-1945
  www.billnkaz.demon.co.uk/droymem2.htm

Grange over Sands
- Grange-Over-Sands War Memorial
  homepage.ntlworld.com/howard.martin/Grange1.html

Great Harwood
- Great Harwood Roll of Honour 1914-1919
  www.btinternet.com/~a.jackson/harwood__af.htm
  Continued on 2 further pages

Huncoat
- Huncoat Roll of Honour 1914-1919
  www.btinternet.com/~a.jackson/huncoat.htm

Hurst
- To the men of Hurst who gave their lives for King and country during the Great War of 1914 to 1918
  www.certificates.fsnet.co.uk/Hurst%20War%20Memorial.htm

Lancaster
- Saint George's Mission Church Roll of Honour
  www.priory.lancs.ac.uk/St.G__roh.html
  At Lancaster

Liverpool
- The Liverpool Scottish First World War Roll of Honour
  www.liverpoolscottish.org.uk/remembook1.htm

Maghull
- War Memorial: St. Andrew's School, Maghull, Merseyside
  www.cus.cam.ac.uk/~jry20/warmem.htm
  World War I

Manchester
- The Manchester Regiment in the Boer War 1899-1902
  www.certificates.fsnet.co.uk/the%20manchester%20regiment.htm
  Includes list of casualties

Oswaldtwistle
- Oswaldtwistle Roll of Honour 1914-1919
  www.btinternet.com/~a.jackson/oswaldtwistle__ah.htm
  Continued at **/oswaldtwistle__iz.htm**

Reddish
- Carls Cam Memorials: War Memorial, south Reddish, Lancashire
  www.carlscam.com/warmem/reddishs.htm
  World War I

Rishton
- Rishton Roll of Honour 1914-1919
  www.btinternet.com/~a.jackson/rishton__ak.htm
  Continued at **/rishton__lz.htm**

Ulverston
- Ulverston War Memorial
  gye.future.easyspace.com/UlvWar.htm
  World War I

- Ulverston War Memorial
  www.rootsweb.com/~england/Memorial.html

Upton
- Upton War Memorial
  www.users.globalnet.co.uk/~pardos/Upton Main.html
  World War I

Withy Grove
- Carls Cam Memorials: War Memorial, Withy Grove, Manchester,
  Lancashire
  www.carlscam.com/warmem/withygrove.htm
  World Wars I & II. Memorial to print workers who lost their lives.

Leicestershire

General
- Lest We Forget: a record of the fallen of Leicestershire & Rutland in
  the Great War
  lrfhs.org.uk/Lestwf.html
  Brief note on a projected publication
- War Memorial Photographs and Transcriptions from Leicester,
  Leicestershire & Rutland
  www.capefam.freeserve.co.uk/lrmems.htm
- The Crimea Casualty List's for the 17th (the Leicestershire) Regiment
  of Foot
  www.cape.fam.freeserve.co.uk/crileic.htm
- The Prince Albert's Own Leicestershire Yeomanry Regiment Memorial
  at Bradgate Park, Leicestershire
  www.capefam.freeserve.co.uk/brdgte1.html
  Boer War, World Wars I & II
- Boer War Casualty Rolls: the Leicestershire Regiment
  www.militarybadges.org.uk/boercas.htm

Ashby de la Zouche
- Ashby de la Zouche, Leicestershire W.W.I.Memorial
  www.capefam.freeserve.co.uk/ashby.htm

Bardon
- The War Memorial of Bardon, Leicestershire
  www.militarybadges.org.uk/leicmemorial/bardon.htm
  World Wars I & II

Barlestone
- The War Memorial of Barlestone, Leicestershire
  www.militarybadges.org.uk/leicmemorial/barlstn.htm
  World Wars I & II

Belton
- Belton War Memorial
  www.militarybadges.org.uk/leicmemorial/belton.htm
  World War I

Birstall

- Birstall War Memorial
  www.militarybadges.org.uk/leicmemorial/bstall.htm
  World Wars I & II

- Birstall War Memorial, Leicester. (St. James's Church)
  www.militarybadges.org.uk/leicmemorial/bstall.htm
  World Wars I & II

Burbage

- Burbage, Leicestershire, War Memorial, 1914-1919
  www.hesketha.freeserve.co.uk/wwi/memorials/burbage.htm

Desford

- Desford War Memorial, Leicestershire
  www.capefam.freeserve.co.uk/dsford.htm
  World Wars I & II

Enderby

- War Memorial, W.W.I.
  www.enderbyheritage.org.uk/RoH.htm
  For Enderby

- War Memorial, W.W.2.
  www.enderbyheritage/rohww2.htm

- Memorial II
  www.enderbyheritage.org.uk/memorial%20II.htm
  Enderby graves elsewhere in the UK

- Memorial III
  www.enderbyheritage.org.uk/memorial%20III.htm
  Enderby graves overseas, World War I

- Memorial IV
  www.enderbyheritage.org.uk/memorial%20IV.htm
  Enderby graves overseas, World War II

Great Glenn

- Great Glenn War Memorial, (Leicestershire, England).
  freepages.genealogy.rootsweb.com/~militaryimages/ggmem.htm

- Great Glen War Memorial and Chesterfield House
  homepage.ntlworld.com/max.matthews/page06d.htm

Hathern

- Hathern War Memorial
  www.militarybadges.org.uk/leicmemorial/hathern.htm
  World Wars I & II, *etc.*

Kegworth

- Lest We Forget: Kegworth War Memorials
  www.kegworthvillage.com/memorial.htm

Leicester

The War Memorial at Gilroes Cemetery, Groby Road, Leicester (City)
  www.militarybadges.org.uk/leicmemorial/glrose
  World Wars I & II

- The War Memorial, Victoria Park, Leicester
  www.militarybadges.org.uk/leicmemorial/lmem1.htm
  World War I. Continued on 2 further pages

Lutterworth

- Lutterworth in World War I
  www.thisislutterworth.com/cfm?pageid=122

- Lutterworth in World War 2
  www.thisislutterworth.com/cms.cfm?pageid=123

Market Harborough

- Market Harborough: an East Midlands Town in the First World War
  www.harboro.ndirect.co.uk/index.htm
  Includes some war memorials

Mountsorrell

- Mountsorrel War Memorial, Leicestershire
  www.military badges.org.uk/leicmemorial/sorrel.htm
  World Words I & II

Newbold Verdon

- The War Memorial of Newbold Verdon, Leicestershire
  www.militarybadges.org.uk/leicmemorial/newbold.htm
  World Wars I & II

Plungar

- The War Memorials of Plungar, Leicestershire at St. Helen's Church
  www.capefam.freeserve.co.uk/plungar.htm
  World War I

Quorn/Quorndon

- Memorials
  www.quorndon-mag.org.uk/british_legion/memorials.html
  Quorn memorials, World Wars I & II

- Genealogy: Quorndon Village: the Wars
  www.quorndon.com/genealogy/wars.html
  World Wars I & II

Ravenstone

- The Ravenstone War Memorial, Leicestershire
  www.militarybadges.org.uk/leicmemorial/rvstone.htm
  World War I

Redmile

- War Memorial in Redmile Church
  www.redmile.archive.care4free.net/war-mem.html

Rothley

- Rothley War Memorial, Leicestershire
  www.militarybadges.org.uk/leicmemorial/rothley.htm
  World Wars I & II

Shepshed

- Shepshed War Memorial
  www.militarybadges.org.uk/leicmemorial/shepshed.htm
  World War I

Woodhouse Eaves

- Woodhouse Eaves War Memorial, Leicestershire
  www.capefam.freeserve.co.uk/whouse.htm
  World Wars I & II

- Woodhouse Eaves War Memorial, Leicestershire
  www.militarybadges.org.uk/leicmemorial/whouse.htm

Woolsthorpe

- Woolsthorpe, (near Belvoir Castle, Leicestershire): War Memorial
  www.capefam.freeserve.co.uk/wlsthorp.htm
  World Wars I & II

Lincolnshire

General

- Lincolnshire, England: Memorials and Rolls of Honour
  www.rootsweb.com/~englin/memorials.htm
  Collection of war memorials; individual pages listed by place below

Ashby

- Ashby War Memorial
  www.genuki.org.uk/big/eng/LIN/Ashby/ashby_mem.html

- Ashby War Memorial
  www.rootsweb.com/~englin/mem/ashby.htm
  World War I

Barkston

- Barkston War Memorial
  www.rootsweb.com/~englin/B/Barkston_mem.htm
  World War I

Boston

- Boston War Memorials
  www.rootsweb.com/~englin/B/boston_mem.htm

Gedney Hill

- Roll of Honour: Gedney Hill, Lincolnshire
  www.roll-of-honour.com/Fenlands/GedneyHillMemorial.html
  World Wars I & II

Gosberton

- Gosberton War Memorial
  www.rootsweb.com/~englin/G/gosberton_mem.htm
  World Wars I & II

Grimsby

- Men of Grimsby: a record of their war services 1914-1918
  freespace.virgin.net/fiona.poulton/master.htm
  Not strictly speaking a 'war memorial', but likely to be of equal use

- Grimsby Roll of Honour 1914-1919
  www.rootsweb.com/~englin/mem/grimsby.htm

Holbeach
- Roll of Honour: Holbeach St. Johns, Lincolnshire
  www.roll-of-honour.com/Fenlands/HolbeachStJohnsMemorial.html
  World Wars I & II

Holton le Clay
- Holton-Le-Clay Roll of Honour
  www.rootsweb.com/~englin/mem/holtonleclay.htm
  World War I

Immingham
- What happened to Joe? Immingham's War Dead Remembered
  www.alamo-design.co.uk/joe/index.htm
  Click on 'complete list of names' for dead of World Wars I & II

Kirkby on Bain
- Kirkby on Bain
  www.memorial-lincs.org.uk/kirkby-On-bain.html
  War Memorial

Kirkstead
- Kirkstead
  www.memorial-lincs.org.uk/html/kirkstead.html
  War Memorial

Messingham
- Messingham War Memorial
  www.genuki.org.uk/big/eng/LIN/Messingham/messingham_mem.html
  World War I

- Messingham Memorial
  www.rootsweb.com/~englin/mem/messingham.htm
  World War I

Pinchbeck
- Pinchbeck War Memorial
  www.rootsweb.com/~englin/mem/pinchbeck.htm

Stickford
- Stickford War Memorial
  www.rootsweb.com/~englin/mem/stickford.htm
  World War I

Surfleet
- Surfleet Memorial
  www.rootsweb.com/~englin/mem/surfleet.htm
  World War II

Sutton St. Edmunds
- Roll of Honour: Sutton St. Edmund, Lincolnshire
  www.roll-of-honour.com/Fenlands/SuttonStEdmundMemorial.html
  World Wars I & II

Sutton St. James
- Roll of Honour: Sutton St. James, Lincolnshire
  www.roll-of-honour.com/Fenlands/SuttonStJamesMemorial.html
  World War I

Tathwell
- Tathwell Memorial
  www.rootsweb.com/~englin/mem/tathwell.htm
  World War I

Tetford
- Tetford
  www.memorial-lincs.org.uk/html/tetford.html
  War Memorial

Tydd St. Mary
- Roll of Honour: Tydd St. Mary, Lincolnshire
  www.roll-of-honour.com/Fenlands/TyddStMaryMemorial.html
  World Wars I & II

Woodhall Spa
- Woodhall Spa
  www.memorial-lincs.org.uk/html/woodhall_spa.html
  War Memorial

Wyberton
- Wyberton Memorial
  www.rootsweb.com/~englin/mem/wyberton.htm
  World War II

Norfolk

Aldborough
- Norfolk: Erpingham District: Aldborough: War Memorials: W.W.I.
  www.genealogy.doun.org/transcriptions/
  documents.php?district_id=2&document_id=6781

Antingham
- Norfolk: Erpingham District: Antingham: War Memorials
  www.genealogy.doun.org/transcriptions/
  documents.php?register_id=12&district_id=2&document.type=370
  World Wars I & II

Bacton
- Norfolk: Tunstead & Happing District: Bacton: War Memorials, W.W.I.
  www.genealogy.dou.org/transcriptions/
  documents.php?district_id=22&document_id=12706

Buxton
- Norfolk: Aylsham District: Buxton: War Memorials: W.W.I.
  www.genealogy.doun.org/transcriptions/
  documents.php?district_id=1&document_id=5682

Earsham
- Earsham
  www.stephen-stratford.co.uk/earsham.htm
  World War I

Emneth
- Roll of Honour: Emneth, Norfolk
  www.roll-of-honour.com/Fenlands/EmnethMemorial.html
  World Wars I & II

Great Bircham
- Norfolk: Docking District: Great Bircham: War Memorials
  www.genealogy.doun.org/transcriptions/
  documents.php?district_id=5&document_id=5932
  World War I

- Norfolk: Docking District: Great Bircham: War Memorials
  www.genealogy.doun.org/transcriptions/
  documents.php?district_id=5&document_id=5933
  World War II

Hanworth
- Norfolk: Erpingham District: Hanworth: War Memorials
  www.genealogy.doun.org/transcriptions/
  documents.php?district_id=2&document_id=12691
  World War I

- Norfolk: Erpingham District: Hanworth: War Memorials
  www.genealogy.doun.org/transcriptions/
  documents.php?district_id=2&document_id=12692

Holkham
- Norfolk: Walsingham District: Holkham: War Memorials
  www.genealogy.doun.org/transcriptions/
  documents.php?district_id=23&document_id=9018
  World War I

- Norfolk: Walsingham District: Holkham: War Memorials
  www.genealogy.doun.org/transcriptions/
  documents.php?district_id=23&document_id=9017
  World War II

Marshland Smeeth
See Smeeth

Salters Lode
- Roll of Honour: Salters Lode, Norfolk
  www.roll-of-honour.com/Fenlands/SaltersLodeMemorial.html
  World Wars I & II

Smeeth
- Roll of Honour: Marshland Smeeth and the Fens, Norfolk
  www.roll-of-honour.com/Fenlands/MarshlandSmeethMemorial.html
  World Wars I & II

Sturston
See Tottington

Swanton Novers
- Swanton Novers, Norfolk, England: War Memorial
  ww3.telus.net/swanton_novers/warmem.htm
  World Wars I & II

Terrington St. Clement
- Roll of Honour: Terrington St. Clement, Norfolk
  www.roll-of-honour.com/Fenlands/TerringtonStClementMemorial.html
  World Wars I & II

Terrington St. John
- Roll of Honour: Terrington St. John, Norfolk
  www.roll-of-honour.com/Fenlands/TerringtonStJohnMemorial.html
  World Wars I & II

Thorpe next Norwich
- Norfolk: Blofield District: Thorpe next Norwich: War Memorials, W.W.I.
  www.genealogy.doun.org/transcriptions/
  documents.php?district_id=3&document_id=6785

- Norfolk: Blofield District: Thorpe next Norwich: War Memorials, W.W.2.
  www.genealogy.doun.org/transcriptions/
  documents.php?district_id=3&document_id=6784

Tilney St. Lawrence
- Roll of Honour: Tilney St. Lawrence, Norfolk
  www.roll-of-honour.com/Fenlands/TilneyStLawrenceMemorial.html
  World Wars I & II

Tottington
- Memorials
  www.merton.ukgo.com/page7.html
  World War I memorial to the soldiers of Tottington and Sturston, now
  at Merton

Walpole St. Andrew
- Roll of Honour: Walpole St. Andrew, Norfolk, & Walpole Cross Keys
  www.roll-of-honour.com/Fenlands/WalpoleStAndrewMemorial.html
  World Wars I & II

Walpole Cross Keys
See Walpole St. Andrew

Walpole St. Peter
- Roll of Honour: Walpole St. Peter, Norfolk
  www.roll-of-honour.com/Fenlands/WalpoleStPeterMemorial.html
  World Wars I & II

Walsoken
- Roll of Honour: Walsoken, Norfolk & Cambs
  www.roll-of-honour.com/Fenlands/WalsokenMemorial.html
  World Wars I & II

Welney
- Roll of Honour: Welney, Norfolk
  www.roll-of-honour.com/Fenlands/WelneyMemorial.htm
  World Wars I & II

West Walton
- Roll of Honour: West Walton, Norfolk
  www.roll-of-honour.com/Fenlands/WestWaltonMemorial.html
  World Wars I & II

Northamptonshire

Eye
- Eye War Memorial 1914-1919
  www.pboro-memorial.com/
  Click on title. Also at:
  members.madasafish.com/~davidpatrickgray/Eye.html

Maxey
- Maxey, Peterborough Roll of Honour
  www.roll-of-honour.com/OtherCounties/Maxey.html
  World Wars I & II

Newborough
- Newborough, Peterborough: Roll of Honour
  www.roll-of-honour.com/OtherCounties/Newborough.html
  World War I

Peterborough
- Peterborough Cathedral: Boer War: Roll of Honour
  www.roll-of-honour.com/Cambridgeshire/PeterboroughBoerWar.htm

- Peterborough War Memorial
  www.pboro-memorial.com
  World Wars I & II. Also at:
  members.madasafish.com/~davidpatrickgray/index.html

Northumberland

General
- Index to the Civilian War Dead Roll of Honour for Northumberland, Durham and Yorkshire
  www.genuki.org.uk/big/eng/Indexes/NE__WarDead/
  World War II

  Recording War Memorials in Northumberland
  www.le.ac.uk/hi/LOCAL__HISTORY/Abstracts/brown.html
  Abstract of an article from the *Local historian.*

Allendale
- 1914-1918 War Memorial inside the Lych Gate of the Parish Church of St. Cuthbert, Allendale
  pages.genealogy.rootsweb.com/~rprobert/photos/nbl/allendale/15.ht ml
  Continued at **/16.html**
  For 1939-45, see **/14.html**

Allenheads
- War Memorial, Allenheads
  pages.genealogy.rootsweb.com/≈rprobert/photos/nbl/allenheads/03.htm
  World Wars I & II

Alnmouth
- War Memorial: Alnmouth, St. John, Northumberland
  www.original-indexes.demon.co.uk/NBL/ALK/WMALKASJ.htm
  World Wars I & II

Amble
- War Memorial: Amble, St. Cuthbert, Northumberland
  www.original-indexes.demon.co.uk/NBL/ALK/WMALKAMB.htm
  World War I

Ancroft
- War Memorial: Ancroft, St. Arne, Northumberland
  www.original-indexes.demon.co.uk/NBL/NHM/WMNHMANC.htm

Belford
- War Memorial: Belford, Northumberland
  www.original-indexes.demon.co.uk/NBL/BAM/WMBAMBFD.htm
  World Wars I & II

Bellingham
- War Memorial: Bellingham, St. Cuthbert, Northumberland
  www.original-indexes.demon.co.uk/NBL/BEL/WMBELBEL.htm
  World War I

Berwick
- War Memorial: Berwick, St. Mary
  www.original-indexes.demon.co.uk/NBL/NHM/WMNHMBSM.htm
  World War I

  War Memorial: Berwick, Holy Trinity, Northumberland
  www.original-indexes.demon.co.uk/NBL/NHM/WMNHMBUT.htm

Branxton
- War Memorial: Branxton, St. Paul
  www.original-indexes.demon.co.uk/NBL/NHM/WMNHMBRX.htm
  World War I

Byker
- War Memorial: Byker, St. Silas, Northumberland
  www.original-indexes.demon.co.uk/NBL/NTE/WMNTEBSS.htm
  World War I

Brunswick
- War Memorial: Brunswick Village, St. Cuthbert, Northumberland
  www.original-indexes.demon.co.uk/NBL/NTC/WMNTCBSC.htm

Cambois
- War Memorial: Cambois, St. Andrew, Northumberland
  www.original-indexes.demon.co.uk/NBL/BED/WMBEDCSA.htm
  World War I

Carham
- War Memorial: Carham, Northumberland
  www.original-indexes.demon.co.uk/NBL/NHM/WMNHMCAR.htm
  World Wars I & II

Chevington
- War Memorial: Chevington, St. John, Northumberland
  www.original-indexes.co.uk/NBL/ALK/WMALKCHV.htm
  World Wars I & II

Chollerton
- War Memorial, Chollerton, St. Giles
  www.original-indexes.demon.co.uk/NBL/BEL/WMBELCHO.htm
  World War II

Corbridge
- War Memorial: Corbridge St. Andrew, Northumberland
  www.original-indexes.demon.co.uk/NBL/COR/WMCORCOR.htm
  World War I

Cornhill
- War Memorial, Cornhill
  www.original-indexes.demon.co.uk/NBL/WMNHMCHL.htm
  World Wars I & II

Corsenside
- War Memorial: Corsenside, St. Cuthbert
  www.original-indexes.demon.co.uk/NBL/BEL/WMBELCSD.htm
  World Wars I & II

Denwick
- War Memorial: Denwick Chapel, Northumberland
  www.original-indexes.demon.co.uk/NBL/WMALKDEN.htm

Dinnington
- War Memorial: Dinnington St. Matthew, Northumberland
  www.original-indexes.demon.co.uk/NBL/NTC/WMNTCDNT.htm
  World Wars I & II

Doddington
- War Memorial: Doddington St. Mary & Michael, Northumberland
  www.original-indexes.demon.co.uk/NBL/BAM/WMBAMDOD.html
  World War I

Dudley

- War Memorial: Dudley, Northumberland
  www.original-indexes.demon.co.uk/NBL/BED/WMBEDDUD.htm
  World Wars I & II

Etal

- War Memorial: Etal, St. Mary, Northumberland
  www.original-indexes.demon.co.uk/NBL/NHM/WMNHMETA.htm
  World War I

Ford

- War Memorial: Ford, St. Michael & All Angels, Northumberland
  www.original-indexes.demon.co.uk/NBL/NHM/WMNHMFOR.htm
  World Wars I & II

Greenhead

- War Memorial: Greenhead, Northumberland
  www.original-indexes.demon.co.uk/NBL/HEX/WMHEXGHD.htm
  World Wars I & II

Haydon Bridge

- War Memorial: Haydon Bridge, St. Cuthbert, Northumberland
  www.original-indexes.demon.co.uk/NBL/HEX/WMHEXHBR.htm
  World Wars I & II

Heddon on the Wall

- War Memorial: Memorial Garden, Heddon on the Wall, Northumberland
  www.original-indexes.demon.co.uk/NBL/COR/WMCORHED.htm

Hexham

- War Memorial: Hexham, Northumberland
  www.original-indexes.demon.co.uk/NBL/HEX/WMHEXHEX.htm
  World Wars I & II

Horncliffe

- War Memorial: Horncliffe, Northumberland
  www.original-indexes.demon.co.uk/NBL/NHM/WMNHMHOR.htm
  World Wars I & II

Horsley

- Horsley War Memorial
  www.swinhope.demon.co.uk/genuki/NBL/Ovingham/HorsleyWarMem.html
  World Wars I & II

Kirkhaugh

- War Memorial: Kirkhaugh, Holy Paraclete, Northumberland
  www.original-indexes.demon.co.uk/NBL/HEX/WMHEXKHG.htm
  World War I

- Kirkhaugh, Holy Paraclete: War Memorial
  www.swinhope.demon.co.uk/genuki/NBL/Kirkhaugh/Kirkhaugh2.html
  World War I

Longbenton

- War Memorial: Longbenton St. Bartholomew, Northumberland
  www.original-indexes.demon.co.uk/NBL/NTE/WMNTELBN.htm
  World War I

Longhirst

- War Memorial: Longhirst, Northumberland
  www.original-indexes.demon.co.uk/NBL/MOR/WMMORLON.htm
  World Wars I & II

Lowick

- War Memorial: Lowick, Northumberland
  www.original-indexes.demon.co.uk/NBL/NHM/WMNHMLOW.htm
  World Wars I & II

Matfen

- War Memorial: Matfen, Northumberland
  www.original-indexes.demon.co.uk/NBL/COR/WMCORMAT.htm
  World Wars I & II

Mickley

- War Memorial: Mickley, St. George
  www.original-indexes.demon.co.uk/NBL/COR/WMCORMIC.htm
  World Wars I & II

Morpeth

- War Memorial: Morpeth, Northumberland
  www.original-indexes.demon.co.uk/NBL/MOR/WMMORMOR.htm
  World Wars I & II

New Hartley
- War Memorial: New Hartley, St. Michael & All Angels, 1939-1945
  www.original-indexes.demon.co.uk/NBL/BED/WMBEDNHA.htm

Newbrough
- War Memorial: Newbrough, St. Peter's, Northumberland
  www.original-indexes.demon.co.uk/NBL/HEX/WMHEXNBR.htm

Newcastle upon Tyne
- War Memorial: Newcastle St. John, Northumberland
  www.original-indexes.demon.co.uk/NBL/NTC/WMNTCNSJ.htm
  World War I

- War Memorial: Newcastle St. Nicholas, Northumberland
  www.original-indexes.demon.co.uk/NBL/NTC/WMNTCNSN.htm
  World War I

- War Memorial: Newcastle, St. Thomas, Northumberland
  www.original-indexes.demon.co.uk/NBL/NTC/WMNTCNST.htm
  World Wars I & II

- War Memorial: University of Newcastle School of Medicine
  www.original-indexes.demon.co.uk/NBL/NTC/WMNTCUNI.htm

Norham
- War Memorial: Norham, St. Cuthbert, Northumberland
  www.original-indexes.demon.co.uk/NBL/NHM/WMNHMNHM.htm
  World Wars I & II

North Gosforth
- War Memorial: North Gosforth Sacred Heart R.C., Northumberland
  www.original-indexes.demon.co.uk/NBL/NTE/WMNTENGO.htm

Riding Mill
- War Memorial: Riding Mill, St. James
  www.original-indexes.demon.co.uk/NBL/COR/WMCORRID.htm
  World Wars I & II

St. John Lee
- War Memorial: St. John Lee, St. John of Beverley, Northumberland
  www.original-indexes.demon.co.uk/NBL/HEX/WMHEXSJL.htm
  World Wars I & II

Seaton Burn
- War Memorial: Seaton Burn, Northumberland
  www.original-indexes.demon.co.uk/NBL/NTE/WMNTESEA.htm
  World Wars I & II

Shotley
- War Memorial: Shotley St. John, Northumberland
  www.original-indexes.demon.co.uk/NBL/COR/WMCORSLQ.htm
  World Wars I & II

Spittal
- War Memorial: Spittal, St. John, Northumberland
  www.original-indexes.demon.co.uk/NBL/NHM/WMNHMSPI.htm
  World War I

Throckley
- War Memorial: Throckley, St. Mary, Northumberland
  www.original-indexes.demon.co.uk/NBL/NTW/WMNTWTHO.htm
  World War I

Tweedmouth
- War Memorial: Tweedmouth, Northumberland
  www.original-indexes.demon.co.uk/NBL/NHM/WMNHMTWM.htm
  World War I and Falklands War

Tynemouth
- War Memorial: Tynemouth, Northumberland
  www.original-indexes.demon.co.uk/NBL/TYN/WMTYNTYN.htm

Ulgham
- War Memorial: Ulgham St. John, Northumberland
  www.original-indexes.demon.co.uk/NBL/MOR/WMMORULG.htm
  World War I

Wall
- War Memorial: Wall, Northumberland
  www.original-indexes.demon.co.uk/NBL/BEL/WMBELWAL.htm

Wark
- War Memorial: Wark, Northumberland
  www.original-indexes.demon.co.uk/NBL/BEL/WMBELWRK.htm
  World War I & II

Warkworth
- War Memorial: Warkworth, Northumberland
  www.original-indexes.demon.co.uk/NBL/ALK/WMALKWKW.htm
  World Wars I & II

Wooler
- War Memorial: Wooler, St. Mary
  www.original-indexes.demon.co.uk/NBL/BAM/WMBAMWLR.htm
  World Wars I & II

Nottinghamshire

General
- Southwell DAC Church History Project
  southwellchurches.nottingham.ac.uk/
  Includes pages of war memorial information, individually listed below

Barnby
- Barnby War Memorials
  www.barnby-in-the-willows.org.uk/Barnby%20War%20Memorials.htm
  World Wars I & II

Burton Joyce
- Burton Joyce St. Helen War Memorial
  southwellchurches.nottingham.ac.uk/b01/hwarmem.html
  World War I

Daybrook
- Daybrook St. Paul War Memorial
  southwellchurches.nottingham.ac.uk/d01/hwarmem.html
  World War I

Gedling
- Gedling All Hallows War Memorials
  southwellchurches.nottingham.ac.uk/g01/hwarmem.html
  World Wars I & II

Lambley
- Lambley Holy Trinity War Memorial
  southwellchurches.nottingham.ac.uk/l01/hwarmem.html
  World Wars I & II

Mansfield
- Mansfield: those who have died on active service
  www.genuki.org.uk/big/eng/Notts/Transcriptions/warmems2.html

New Basford
- New Basford St. Augustine War Memorial
  southwellchurches.nottingham.ac.uk/b03/hwarmem.html
  Boer War, World Wars I & II

Nottingham
Nottingham St. Peter War Memorials
southwellchurches.nottingham.ac.uk/n01/hwarmem.html
World War I

Shireoaks
- Shireoaks St. Luke War Memorial
southwellchurches.nottingham.ac.uk/s02/hwarmem.html
World Wars I & II

Rutland

General
- Commonwealth War Graves Commission Headstones in Rutland
www.users.globalnet.co.uk/~shelvey/headstones.htm
Collection; some pages separately listed below

- The War Memorials of Rutland
www.users.globalnet.co.uk/~shelvey/villages.htm
Collection; individual pages separately listed below

- The Rutland War Memorial Pages
www.capefam.freeserve.co.uk/memorial2.htm

Ashwell
- Ashwell
www.users.globalnet.co.uk/~shelvey/ashwell1.htm
War Memorial

Barleythorpe
See Langham

Belton
- Belton-in-Rutland
www.users.globalnet.co.uk/~shelvey/belton1.htm
World War I

Burley on the Hill
- Burley-on-the-Hill
www.users.globalnet.co.uk/~shelvey/burley.htm
World War I

Caldecott
- Caldecott
www.users.globalnet.co.uk/~shelvey/web%20page%202/caldecott1.htm
World War I

Clipsham
- Clipsham
www.users.globalnet.co.uk/~shelvey/clipsham1.htm
World War I

Cottesmore

- Cottesmore
  www.users.globalnet.co.uk/~shelvey/cottesmore1.htm
  World War I
  See also Morcott

Edith Weston

- Edith Weston (Rutland) War Memorial
  www.capefam.freeserve.co.uk/memor4.htm

Empingham

- Empingham
  www.users.globalnet.co.uk/~shelvey/empingham1.htm
  World War I
  See also Ketton

Essendine

- Essendine
  www.users.globalnet.co.uk/~shelvey/essendine1.htm
  World Wars I & II

Exton

See Greetham

Great Casterton

- Great Casterton
  www.users.globalnet.co.uk/~shelvey/gcasterton1.htm
  World Wars I & II
  See also Ketton

Greetham

- Greetham (2) and Exton (2)
  www.users.globalnet.co.uk/~shelvey/greetham.exton.html
  Commonwealth War Graves Commission headstones

Ketton

- Ketton
  www.users.globalnet.co.uk/~shelvey/ketton1.htm
  World Wars I & II

- Ketton (Rutland) War Memorial
  www.capefam.freeserve.co.uk/memor2.htm
  Also includes Empingham and Great Casterton War Memorials

Langham

- Langham and Barleythorpe
  www.users.globalnet.co.uk/~shelvey/langham1.htm
  World War I

Lyddington

- Lyddington
  www.users.globalnet.co.uk/~shelvey/lyddington1.htm
  World Wars I & II

Lyndon

- Lyndon (Rutland) War Memorial
  www.capefam.freeserve.co.uk/memor5.htm
  Also includes Whitwell and Wing War Memorials

Manton

- Manton
  www.users.globalnet.co.uk/~shelvey/manton1.htm
  World Wars I & II

Market Overton

- Market Overton
  www.users.globalnet.co.uk/~shelvey/market%20Overton1.htm
  Continued at **/marketoverton2.htm**
  World Wars I & II

Morcott

- Morcott
  www.globalnet.co.uk/~shelvey/morcott1.htm
  World War I

- Keith Shelvey's Rutland War Memorials Project
  www.capefam.freeserve.co.uk/memorials.htm
  Includes inscriptions from Morcott and Cottesmore

North Luffenham

- North Luffenham
  www.users.globalnet.co.uk/~shelvey/north%20%luffenham%202.htm

- North Luffenham
  www.users.globalnet.co.uk/~shelvey/northluffenham1.htm
  World War I

- North Luffenham (Rutland) War Memorial
  www.capefam.freeserve.co.uk/memor6.htm
  Also includes Ridlington War Memorial

Preston
- Preston
  www.users.globalnet.co.uk/~shelvey/preston1.htm
  World Wars I & II

Ridlington
  See North Luffenham

Ryhall
- Ryhall
  www.users.globalnet.co.uk/~shelvey/ryhall.htm
  World Wars I & II

Seaton
- Seaton
  www.users.globalnet.co.uk/~shelvey/seaton1.htm
  World War I

Tickencote
- Tickencote
  www.users.globalnet.co.uk/~shelvey/tickencote1.htm
  World War I

Tinwell
- Tinwell (Rutland) War Memorial
  www.capefam.freeserve.co.uk/memor3.htm

Uppingham
- Uppingham
  www.users.globalnet.co.uk/~shelvey/uppingham.html
  Commonwealth War Graves Commission headstones

Whissendine
- Whissendine
  www.users.globalnet.co.uk/~shelvey/whissendine1.htm
  World Wars I & II

Whitwell
- Whitwell
  www.users.globalnet.co.uk/=shelvey/whitwell.htm
  War Memorial
  See also Lyndon

Wingwar
See Lyndon

Staffordshire

Bilston
- Bilston, Willenhall and Darlaston
  www.warmem.pwp.blueyonder.co.uk/bils-dar.htm
  War Memorials

Bushbury
- Bushbury, Wednesfield and Heath Town
  www.warmem.pwp.blueyonder.co.uk/bush-wed.htm
  War Memorial

Darlaston
See Bilston

Heath Town
See Bushbury

Hurst Hill
- St. Mary's, Hurst Hill War Memorial
  www.sedgleymanor.com/churches/c__of__e/
      hurst__hill__st__marys__church__war__memorial__1.jpg
  Continued on 2 further pages

Wednesbury
See Bushbury

Willenhall
See Bilston

Wolverhampton
- War Memorials of Wolverhampton
  www.warmem.pwp.blueyonder.co.uk

Suffolk

General
- Suffolk's Book of Remembrance
  www.suffolkcc.gov.uk/libraries__and__heritage/sro/roh/thebook.html

- Suffolk's Book of Remembrance
  www.suffolkcc.gov.uk/sro/roh/
  World War I

- 11th Battalion, the Suffolk Regiment: Full list of Casualties: 970 names
  www.curme.co.uk/casualts.htm
  World War I

- Roll of Honour: 1st Suffolk Regiment, 6th June 1944
  battlefieldsww2.50megs.com/1st__suffolks__roll-of-honour.htm

- Rod Gibson's Home Page
  www.users.globalnet.co.uk/~rodg/
  Many pages of rolls of honour, separately listed below

Aldeburgh
- Aldeburgh Thumbnails
  www.debenweb.co.uk/suffolkpages/aldeb/index.htm
  Includes photographs of a few sections of this war memorial

Barnardiston
- Barnardiston Roll of Honour
  www.users.globalnet.co.uk/%7Erodg/barn.htm
  World War I

Bawdsey
- [Bawdsey War Memorial]
  www.debenweb.co.uk/suffolkphotos/bawdsey/ww1-hon-roll.jpg
  World Wars I & II

Benhall
- Benhall Thumbnails
  www.debenweb.co.uk/suffolkpages/ben/index.html
  Photos of this war memorial

Brandon
- Brandon at War
  www.btinternet.com/~sgthomer/rollofhonour.htm
  Includes World War I roll of honour

Butley
- [Butley War Memorial]
  www.debenweb.co.uk/suffolkphotos/butley/but11.jpg
  World War I

Earl Soham
- War Memorial
  www.earl-soham.suffolk.gov.uk/genealogy/war__memorial.htm
  Of Earl Soham, World Wars I & II

Exning
- Exning, Suffolk, Roll of Honour
  www.roll-of-honour.com/OtherCounties/Exning.html
  World Wars I & II

Great Wratting
- Great Wratting Roll of Honour
  www.users.globalnet.co.uk/%7Erodg/GtWratting.htm
  World Wars I & II

Hartest
- Hartest Roll of Honour
  www.users.globalnet.co.uk/%7Erodg/hartest.htm
  World Wars I & II

Haverhill
- Haverhill Roll of Honour
  www.users.globalnet.co.uk/%7Erodg/Haverhill.htm
  World Wars I & II

- Old Independent Church Roll of Honour
  www.users.globalnet.co.uk/%7Erodg/OldIndepen.htm
  At Haverhill, World Wars I & II

- Hollesley Thumbnails
  www.debenweb.co.uk/suffolkpages/holl/index.htm
  War memorial photographs

Kedington
- Kedington Roll of Honour
  www.globalnet.co.uk/%7Erodg/Kedington.htm
  Various wars

Little Wratting
- Little Wratting Roll of Honour
  www.users.globalnet.co.uk/%7Erodg/LtlWratting.htm

Long Melford
- Long Melford Roll of Honour
  www.users.globalnet.co.uk/%7Erodg/LongMelford.htm
  World Wars I & II. Also at:
  www.stedmundsbury.anglican.org/longmelford/roll__of__honour.htm

Marlesford
- [Marlesford War Memorial 1914-1918]
  www.debenweb.co.uk/suffolkphotos/marlesford/
  2002churchint4-detail.jpg

Withersfield
- Withersfield Roll of Honour
  www.users.globalnet.co.uk/%7Erodg/Withersfield.htm
  World Wars I & II

Warwickshire

General
- War Memorials of Warwickshire
  members.aol.com/sirobuk/WarMemorialsWebSite/WarMemorials.html
  Collection of web pages, individually listed below

Alveston
- Alveston
  members.aol.com/sirobuk/WarMemorialsWebSite/Parishes/Alveston.html
  World War I

Arrow
- Arrow
  members.aol.com/sirobuk/WarMemorialsWebSite/Parishes/Arrow.html
  World Wars I & II

Aston Cantlow
- St. John the Baptist, Aston Cantlow: War Memorial
  med441.bham.ac.uk/WarMems/astoncantlow.html
  World Wars I & II

Barcheston
- St. Martin's, Barcheston
  med441.bham.ac.uk/WarMems/barcheston.html
  World Wars I & II

Bidford on Avon
- Bidford on Avon: War Memorial
  med441.bham.ac.uk/WarMems/bidford.html
  World Wars I & II

Binton
- Binton
  members.aol.com/sirobuk/WarMemorialsWebSite/Parishes/Binton.html
  World Wars I & II

- St. Peter's, Binton: War Memorial
  med441.bham.ac.uk/WarMems/binton.html
  World Wars I & II

Birmingham
- Roll of Honour for BSA Employees killed in enemy Bombing Raids on Factories 1939-1945
  www.genuki.org.uk/big/eng/WAR/deloyd/BSA193945.html

- Birmingham University: War Memorial
  med441.bham.ac.uk/WarMems/bhamuni.html
  World Wars I & II

Coughton
- St. Peter's, Coughton: War Memorials
  med441.bham.ac.uk/WarMems/coughton.html
  World War I

Darlingscott
- St. George's, Darlingscott: War Memorial
  med441.bham.ac.uk/WarMems/darlingscott.html
  World War I

Dunchurch
- Dunchurch (including Thurlaston)
  members.aol.com/sirobuk/WarMemorialsWebSite/Parishes/Dunchurch.html
  World Wars I & II

Edgbaston
- St. Bartholomew's, Edgbaston Old Church: War Memorial
  med441.bham.ac.uk/WarMems/edgbaston.html
  World Wars I & II

Exhall
- St. Giles, Exhall: War Memorials
  med441.bham.ac.uk/WarMems/exhall.html
  World Wars I & II

Great Wolford
- St. Michael and All Angels, Great Wolford: War Memorial
  med441.bham.ac.uk/WarMems/greatwolford.html
  World Wars I & II

Halford
- St. Mary's, Halford: War Memorials
  med441.bham.ac.uk/WarMems/halford.html
  World War I

Harbury

- Harbury
  members.aol.com/sirobuk/WarMemorialsWebSite/Parishes/Harbury.html
  World Wars I & II

Hockley Heath

- Hockley Heath
  members.aol.com/sirobuk/WarMemorialsWebSite/Parishes/
  HockleyHeath.html
  World Wars I & II

Honington

- All Saints, Honington
  med441.bham.ac.uk/WarMems/honington.html

Ilmington

- Ilmington: War Memorials
  med441.bham.ac.uk/WarMems/ilmington.html
  World Wars I & II

Lapworth

- Lapworth
  members.aol.com/sirobuk/WarMemorialsWebSite/Parishes/Lapworth.html
  World Wars I & II

Little Compton

- St. Denys', Little Compton
  med441.bham.ac.uk/WarMems/littlecompton.html
  World Wars I & II

Long Compton

- St. Peter & St. Paul, Long Compton: War Memorial
  med441.bham.ac.uk/WarMems/longcompton.html
  World War I

Lower Quinton

- Lower Quinton
  members.aol.com/sirobuk/WarMemorialsWebSite/Parishes/
  LowerQuinton.html
  World War I

Loxley

- Loxley
  members.aol.com/sirobuk/WarMemorialsWebSite/Parishes/Loxley.html
  World Wars I & II

Rowington

- Rowington
  members.aol.com/sirobuk/WarMemorialsWebSite/Parishes/
  Rowington.html
  World Wars I & II

Salford Priors

- St. Matthew's, Salford Priors: War Memorial
  med441.bham.ac.uk/WarMems/salfordpriors.html
  World Wars I & II

Sambourne

- Sambourne: War Memorial
  med441.bham.ac.uk/WarMems/sambourne.html
  World War I

Shipston on Stour

- Shipston on Stour
  members.aol.com/sirobuk/WarMemorialsWebSite/Parishes/Shipston.html
  World Wars I & II

Shirley

- Shirley War Memorial
  med441.bham.ac.uk/WarMems/shirley.html
  World Wars I & II

Snitterfield

- Snitterfield
  members.aol.com/sirobuk/WarMemorialsWebSite/Parishes/
  Snitterfield.html
  World Wars I & II

Solihull

- Solihull Area Air Services Casualties
  med441.bham.ac.uk/WarMems/solihullair.html

Southam

- Southam
  members.aol.com/sirobuk/WarMemorialsWebSite/Parishes/Southam.html
  World Wars I & II

Stretton on Fosse

- St. Peter's, Stretton on Fosse: War Memorials
  med441.bham.ac.uk/WarMems/strettonfosse.html
  World Wars I & II

Studley

- Remembering the Great War: Studley, Warwickshire
  www.hellfire-corner.demon.co.uk/Westlakestudley.htm

- Studley
  members.aol.com/sirobuk/WarMemorialsWebSite/Parishes/Studley.html
  World Wars I & II

Sutton Coldfield

- Sutton Coldfield War Memorial
  med441.bham.ac.uk/WarMems/suttoncoldfield.html

Tanworth

- Tanworth
  members.aol.com/sirobuk/WarMemorialsWebSite/Parishes/Tanworth.html
  World Wars I & II

Temple Grafton

- Temple Grafton
  members.aol.com/sirobuk/WarMemorialsWebSite/Parishes/
  TempleGrafton.html
  World Wars I & II

- St. Andrew's, Temple Grafton: War Memorial
  med441.bham.ac.uk/WarMems/templegrafton.html
  World Wars I & II

Thurlaston

See Dunchurch

Ufton

- Ufton
  members.aol.com/sirobuk/WarMemorialsWebSite/Parishes/Ufton.html
  World War I

Ullenhall

- Ullenhall
  members.aol.com/sirobuk/WarMemorialsWebSite/Parishes/Ullenhall.html
  World Wars I & II

Walton

- Walton
  members.aol.com/sirobuk/WarMemorialsWebSite/Parishes/Walton.html
  World Wars I & II

Welford on Avon

- St. Peter's, Welford on Avon: War Memorials
  med441.bham.ac.uk/WarMems/welfordonavon.html

Wellesbourne

- Wellesbourne
  members.aol.com/sirobuk/WarMemorialsWebSite/Parishes/
  Wellesbourne.html

  World Wars I & II, *etc.*

Whatcote

- St. Peter, Whatcote: War Memorials
  med441.bham.ac.uk/WarMems/whatcote.html
  World Wars I & II

Whichford

- St. Michael's, Whichford
  med441.bham.ac.uk/WarMems/whichford.html
  World War I

Wootton Wawen

- Wootton Wawen
  members.aol.com/sirobuk/WarMemorialsWebSite/Parishes/
  WoottonWawen.html

  World Wars I & II

Westmoreland

Brimington
- War Memorials: Brimington War Memorials 1914-1918
  www.skimber.demon.co.uk/brim/brim.htm

Keswick
- [The Keswick War Memorial, 1914-18 and 1939-45]
  www.orrison.com/genealogy/monuments/keswick.html

Windermere
- [Windermere]: War Memorials Search Results Page
  www.war-memorials.org.uk/
  Click on 'Westmorland' and 'Windermere'

Yorkshire

General
- Cenotaphs in the Wakefield Area
  freepages.history.rootsweb.com/~framland/warind.htm
  Collections from various places, separately listed below

- War Memorials in the Wakefield Area: West Riding Constabulary War Memorial
  freepages.history.rootsweb.com/~framland/war.htm
  World Wars I & II. Also at:
  www.wdfhs.co.uk/war.htm

Acaster Malbis
- Acaster Malbis Parish: Acaster Malbis War Memorial Transcription
  www.genuki.org.uk/big/eng/YKS/ARY/AcasterMalbis/
  WMNaburnWM2.html

  World Wars I & II

Ackton Hall
See Featherstone

Ackworth
- Ackworth War Memorial
  www.wdfhs.co.uk/ack.htm

- War Memorials in the Wakefield Area: Ackworth Millenium Memorial
  freepages.history.rootsweb.com/~framland/amm.htm
  World Wars I & II. Also at:
  www.wdfhs.co.uk/amm.htm

Addingham
- Addingham Roll of Honour
  www.donbarrett.pwp.blueyonder.co.uk/war.ww1.htm
  World War I

- Addingham Parish: Addingham Memorial Plaque Transcription
  www.genuki.org.uk/big/eng/YKS/WRY/Addingham/
  MPAddinghamWM__Mosaic.html
  World Wars I & II. See also:
  /MPAddinghamStPeterWMPlaque__1.html

Allerton Bywater

- War Memorials in the Wakefield Area: Allerton Bywater War Memorial
  freepages.history.rootsweb.com/~framland/all.htm
  Also at: **www.wdfhs.co.uk/all.htm**

Altofts

- War Memorials in the Wakefield Area: Altofts War Memorial
  freepages.history.rootsweb.com/~framland/alt.htm
  World Wars I & II. Also at:
  www.wdfhs.co.uk/alt.htm

Appleton le Moors

- Lastingham Parish: Appleton le Moors Memorial Plaque Transcription
  www.genuki.org.uk/big/eng/YKS/NRY/Lastingham/
  MPAppletonLeMoorsWM.html
  World War I

Appleton Roebuck

- Bolton Percy Parish: Appleton Roebuck Memorial Plaque Transcription
  www.genuki.org.uk/big/eng/YKS/ARY/Boltonpercy/
  MPAppletonRoebuckWM.html
  World War I

Arncliffe

- Arncliffe Parish: Hubberholme Memorial Plaque Transcription
  www.genuki.org.uk/big/eng/YKS/WRY/Arncliffe/
  MPHubberholmeStMichaelInsideWMPlaque.html
  World War I

- Arncliffe Parish: Arncliffe Memorial Plaque Transcription
  www.genuki.org.uk/big/eng/YKS/WRY/Arncliffe/
  MPArncliffeStOswaldRoH.html
  World War I

- Arncliffe Parish: Arncliffe Memorial Plaque Transcription
  www.genuki.org.uk/big/eng/YKS/WRY/Arncliffe/
  MPArncliffeFloddenFieldNames.html
  Memorial to Arncliffe men who fought at Flodden Field, 1513

Askham Bryan

- Askham Bryan Parish: Askham Bryan War Memorial Transcription
  www.genuki.org.uk/big/eng/YKS/ARY/Askhambryan/
  WMAskhamBryanWM.html

Askrigg

- Aysgarth Parish: Askrigg Roll of Honour Transcription
  www.genuki.org.uk/big/eng/YKS/NRY/Aysgarth/RoHAskriggRoH.html
  World War II

Austwick

- Clapham Parish: Austwick War Memorial Transcription
  www.genuki.org.uk/big/eng/YKS/WRY/Clapham/
  WMAustwickCemeteryWM__0.html
  World Wars I & II

- Clapham Parish: Austwick Roll of Honour Transcription
  www.genuki.org.uk/big/eng/YKS/WRY/Clapham/
  RoHAustwickTheEpiphanyROH.html
  World Wars I & II

Badsworth

- War Memorials in the Wakefield Area: Memorial Board in the Church
  of St. Mary, Badsworth
  freepages.history.rootsweb.com/~framland/smb.htm
  World War I

Barkisland

- Barkisland War Memorial
  www.hamm25.freeserve.co.uk/BarkMem.htm

Barnoldswick

- Thornton in Lonsdale Parish: Barnoldswick War Memorial
  Transcriptions
  www.genuki.org.uk/big/eng/YKS/WRY/Thorntoninlonsdale/
  WMBarnoldswickWM__0.html
  World Wars I & II

Barton le Street

Barton Le Street Parish: Barton le Street Roll of Honour Transcription
www.genuki.org.uk/big/eng/YKS/NRY/Bartonlestreet/RoH/
BartonLeStreetRoH.html
World War I

Batley

- Batley Parish: Gildersome War Memorial Transcription
  www.genuki.org.uk/big/eng/YKS/WRY/Batley/WMGildersomeDummy.html
  World War I

Beeford

- Beeford Parish: Beeford War Memorial Transcription
  www.genuki.org.uk/big/eng/YKS/ERY/Beeford/WMBeefordWM1.html

Ben Rhydding

- Ilkley Parish: Ben Rhydding Memorial Plaque Transcription
  www.genuki.org.uk/big/eng/YKS/WRY/Ilkley/
  MPBenRhyddingStJohnSingleWMPlaque.html
  World War I

- Ilkley Parish: Ben Rhydding Memorial Plaque Transcription
  www.genuki.org.uk/big/eng/YKS/WRY/Ilkley/
  MPBenRhyddingStJohnWMPlaques.html
  World Wars I & II

Bielby

- Hayton Parish: Bielby War Memorial Transcription
  www.genuki.org.uk/big/eng/YKS/ERY/Hayton/WMBielbyWM1.html
  World Wars I & II

Bilsdale Midcable

- Helmsley Parish: Bilsdale Midcable Memorial Plaque Transcription
  www.genuki.org.uk/big/eng/YKS/NRY/Helmsley/
  MPBilsdaleMidcableFangdaleWMPlaque.html
  World War I

Bishop Wilton

- Bishop Wilton Parish: Bishop Wilton War Memorial Transcription
  www.genuki.org.uk/big/eng/YKS/ERY/Bishopwilton/
  WMBishopWiltonWM1.html

Bolsterstone

- [Bolsterstone War Memorial]
  www.bolsterstone.de/War%20Memorial.htm
  World War I

Bolton by Bowland

- Bolton by Bolland Parish: Bolton by Bolland War Memorial
  Transcription
  www.genuki.org.uk/big/eng/YKS/WRY/Boltonbybolland/WM/
  BoltonByBowlandWM__0.html
  World Wars I & II

Bolton by Bolland Parish

- Bolton by Bolland Parish: Bolton by Bolland Memorial Plaque
  Transcription
  www.genuki.org.uk/big/eng/YKS/WRY/Boltonbybolland/
  MPBoltonByBowlandWM__0.html
  World War I

Bolton Percy

- Bolton Percy Parish: Bolton Percy War Memorial Transcription
  www.genuki.org.uk/big/eng/YKS/ARY/Boltonpercy/
  WMBoltonPercyWM.html

See also Appleton Roebuck

Bolton upon Swale

- Catterick Parish: Bolton upon Swale Memorial Plaque Transcription
  www.genuki.org.uk/big/eng/YKS/NRY/Catterick/
  MPBoltonOnSwaleRoH.html

  World Wars I & II

Bossall

- Bossall Parish: Bossall Memorial Plaque Transcription
  www.genuki.org.uk/big/eng/YKS/NRY/Bossall/MPBossallWM.html
  World Wars I & II

Bowers Allerton

- War Memorials in the Wakefield Area: Bowers Allerton War Memorial
  freepages.history.rootsweb.com/~framland/bow.htm
  World Wars I & II. Also at:
  www.wdfhs.co.uk/bow.htm

Bradshaw

- Bradshaw War Memorial
  www.hamm25.freeserve.co.uk/BradMem.htm

Bridlington

- Bridlington Parish: Bridlington Roll of Honour Transcription
  www.genuki.org.uk/big/eng/YKS/ERY/Bridlington/
  ROHBridlingtonWM1.html

  World Wars I & II

- Bridlington Parish: Bridlington Memorial Plaque Inscription
  www.genuki.org.uk/big/eng/YKS/ERY/Bridlington/
  MPBridlingtonChristChurchWMplaque14-18.html
  At Christ Church, 1914-18

- Bridlington Parish: Bridlington Memorial Plaque
  www.genuki.org.uk/big/eng/YKS/ERY/Bridlington/
  MPBridlingtonChristChurchWMplaque39-45.html
  In Christ Church, 1939-45

- Bridlington Parish: Bridlington Memorial Plaque Transcription
  www.genuki.org.uk/big/eng/YKS/ERY/Bridlington/MPBridPrioryWM1.html
  In Priory church, 1914-19

- Bridlington Parish: Bridlington Memorial Plaque Transcription
  www.genuki.org.uk/big/eng/YKS/ERY/Bridlington/
  MPBridlingtonTrinityROH.html
  In Trinity Church, 1914-18

Broomfleet

- South Cave Parish: Broomfleet War Memorial Transcription
  www.genuki.org.uk/big/eng/YKS/ERY/Southcave/WBroomfleetWM.html
  World War I

Brompton

- The Brompton War Memorial
  www.scmetcalfe.btinternet.co.uk/pages/brlist.htm

Brotton

- Brotton Parish: Brotton War Memorial Transcription
  www.genuki.org.uk/big/eng/YKS/NRY/Brotton/WMBrottonWM.html

Bubwith

- Bubwith Parish: Bubwith War Memorial Transcription
  www.genuki.org.uk/big/eng/YKS/ERY/Bubwith/WMBubwithWM1.html
  World Wars I & II

Burton Agnes

- Burton Agnes Parish: Burton Agnes Roll of Honour Transcription
  www.genuki.org.uk/big/eng/YKS/ERY/Burtonagnes/
  RoHBurtonAgnesRoH.html
  World War I

Burton Fleming

- Burtonfleming: Burtonfleming War Memorial Transcription
  www.genuki.org.uk/big/eng/YKS/ERY/Burtonfleming/
  WMBurtonFlemingWM.html
  World War I

Burton in Lonsdale

- Thornton in Lonsdale Parish: Burton in Lonsdale War Memorial Transcription
  www.genuki.org.uk/big/eng/YKS/WRY/Thorntoninlonsdale/
  WMBurtonInLonsdaleWM__0.html
  World War I

Burton Pidsea

- Burton Pidsea Parish: Burton Pidsea Roll of Honour Transcription
  www.genuki.org.uk/big/eng/YKS/ERY/Burtonpidsea/
  RoHBurtonPidseaRoH.html
  World Wars I & II

Calderdale

- Calderdale War Memorials
  www.hamm25.freeserve.co.uk/
  Collection of web pages, individually listed here

Calverley

- Calverley Parish: Calverley War Memorial Transcription
  www.genuki.org.uk/big/eng/YKS/WRY/Calverley/
  WMCalverleyDummy.html
  World War I

- Calverley War Memorial
  www.calverley.info/calv__ceno.htm
  World Wars I & II

Carleton

- War Memorials in the Wakefield Area: Carleton War Memorial
  freepages.history.rootsweb.com/~framland/care.htm
  World War I. Also at:
  www.wdfhs.co.uk/care.htm

Carlton

- War Memorials in the Wakefield Area: Carlton War Memorial
  freepages.history.rootsweb.com/~framland/car.htm
  World Wars I & II. Also at:
  www.wdfhs.co.uk/car.htm

Carnaby
- Carnaby Parish: Carnaby Memorial Plaque Transcription
www.genuki.org.uk/big/eng/YKS/ERY/Carnaby/MPCarnabyRoH3.html
World War I

Castleford
- War Memorials in the Wakefield Area: All Saints Church, Castleford.
Provisional List from Newspaper 1914-1918
freepages.history.rootsweb.com/≈framland/caspc.htm
Also at: **www.wdfhs.co.uk/caspc.htm**

- Castleford War Memorial
www.wdfhs.co.uk/cas.htm

Chop Gate
- Helmsley Parish: Chop Gate War Memorial Transcription
www.genuki.org.uk/big/eng/YKS/NRY/Helmsley/
WMChopGateWarMemorial__0.html
World War I

Clapham
- Clapham Parish: Clapham War Memorial Transcription
www.genuki.org.uk/big/eng/YKS/WRY/Clapham/
WMClaphamWM__0.html
World War I

Clayton
- Garden adjacent to Clayton Hospital
www.wdfhs.co.uk/clay2.htm

- Plaque in the Clayton Hospital Nurses Hostel
www.wdfhs.co.uk/clay.htm

Clifton
- Clifton War Memorial
www.hamm25.freeserve.co.uk/clifmem.htm

Cold Kirby
- Cold Kirby Parish: Cold Kirby Memorial Plaque Transcription
www.genuki.org.uk/big/eng/YKS/NRY/Coldkirby/MPColdKirbyRoH.html
World War I

Coley
- Halifax Parish: Coley Memorial Plaque Transcriptions
www.genuki.org.uk/big/eng/YKS/WRY/Halifax/MPColeyStJohnWM.html
World War I

Coniston
- Gargrave Parish: Coniston Cold War Memorial Transcription
www.genuki.org.uk/big/eng/YKS/WRY/Gargrave/
WMConistonColdWM__0.html
World War I

Cononley
- Kildwick Parish: Cononley Memorial Plaque Transcriptions
www.genuki.org.uk/big/eng/YKS/WRY/Kildwick/
MPCononleySideOfInstituteWMPlaque.html
World Wars I & II

Cornholme
- Rochdale Parish: Cornholme War Memorial Transcription
www.genuki.org.uk/big/eng/YKS/WRY/Rochdale/
WMCornholmeWM__0.html

Cowling
- Kildwick Parish: Cowling War Memorial Transcription
www.genuki.org.uk/big/eng/YKS/WRY/Kildwick/
WMCowlingHolyTrinityWithWM.html
World Wars I & II

Crigglestone
- War Memorials in the Wakefield Area: Crigglestone War Memorial
freepages.history.rootsweb.com/~framland/cri.htm
World War II. Also at:
www.wdfhs.co.uk/cri.htm

Crofton
- War Memorials in the Wakefield Area: Crofton War Memorial
freepages.history.rootsweb.com/~framland/crof.htm
Also at: **freepages.history.rootsweb.com/~framland/smcroft.htm**

- Crofton War Memorial
www.wdfhs.co.uk/crof.htm

Darrington

- Darrington War Memorial
  www.wdfhs.co.uk/dar.htm

Denby Dale

- Penistone Parish: Denby Dale War Memorial Transcription
  www.genuki.org.uk/big/eng/YKS/WRY/Penistone/
  WMDenbyDaleWM__0.html
  World Wars I & II

Denshaw

- Rochdale Parish: Denshaw War Memorial Transcription
  www.genuki.org.uk/big/eng/YKS/WRY/Rochdale/
  WMDenshawWM__0.html
  World Wars I & II

Dinnington

- Dinnington War Memorial Names
  www.milners28.freeserve.co.uk/dinnington/dinnington__war__names.htm
  World War II

Dunnington

- Dunnington Parish: Dunnington Memorial Plaque Transcription
  www.genuki.org.uk/big/eng/YKS/ERY/Dunnington/MPDunningtonWM.html
  World War I

Dunscroft

- Hatfield Parish: Dunscroft Memorial Plaque Transcription
  www.genuki.org.uk/big/eng/YKS/WRY/Hatfield/
  MPDunscroftStEdwinWMPlaque.html
  World War I

Dunsdale

- [Dunsdale]: War Memorials Search Results Page
  www.war-memorials.org.uk/
  Click on 'Cleveland' and 'Dunsdale'

Dunsop

- Slaidburn Parish: Dunsop Bridge War Memorial Transcription
  www.genuki.org.uk/big/eng/YKS/WRY/Slaidburn/
  WMDunsopBridgeWM__0.html
  World War I

Easington

- Easington Parish: Easington Memorial Plaque Transcription
  www.genuki.org.uk/big/eng/YKS/ERY/Easington/MPEasingtonRoH1.html
  World Wars I & II

East Ayton

- Seàmer Parish: East Ayton War Memorial Transcription
  www.genuki.org.uk/big/eng/YKS/NRY/Seamer/WMEastAytonWM1.html
  World Wars I & II

East Cowick

- Snaith Parish: East Cowick War Memorial Transcriptions
  www.genuki.org.uk/big/eng/YKS/WRY/Snaith/WMEastCowickWM2.html

East Hardwick

- War Memorials in the Wakefield Area: East Hardwick War Memorial
  freepages.history.rootsweb.com/~framland/char.htm
  World Wars I & II. Also at:
  www.wdfhs.co.uk/ehar.htm

East Marton

- East Marton Parish: East Marton Roll of Honour Transcription
  www.genuki.org.uk/big/eng/YKS/WRY/Eastmarton/
  RoHEastMartonStPeterROH.html
  World Wars I & II

Elland

- Elland War Memorial
  www.hamm25.freeserve.co.uk/EllandMem.htm

Farnley

- Leeds Parish: Farnley War Memorial Transcriptions
  www.genuki.org.uk/big/eng/YKS/WRY/Leeds/WMFarnleyDummy.html
  World Wars I & II

Farsley

- Calverley Parish: Farsley War Memorial Transcription
  www.genuki.org.uk/big/eng/YKS/WRY/Calverley/WMFarsleyDummy.html
  Boer War 1899-1902

- Farsley: Transcription and additional information for Farsley Cenotaph
  www.genuki.org.uk/big/eng/YKS/Misc/Transcriptions/WRY/
  FarsleyCenotaph.html
  World Wars I & II

Featherstone

- Featherstone War Memorial
  www.wdfhs.co.uk/feat.htm

- Featherstone War Memorial
  www.wdfhs.co.uk/fea.htm
  At Ackton Hall Colliery

Ferrybridge

- War Memorials in the Wakefield Area: Ferrybridge War Memorial
  freepages.history.rootsweb.com/≈framland/fer.htm
  World Wars I & II

- Ferrybridge War Memorial 1914-1918
  www.wdfhs.co.uk/fer.htm

Filey

- Filey Parish: Filey Memorial Plaque Transcription
  www.genuki.org.uk/big/eng/WKS/NRY/Filey/
  MPFileyStOswaldWMplaque1.html
  World War I

- Filey Parish: Filey War Memorial Transcription
  www.genuki.org.uk/big/eng/YKS/NRY/Filey/WMFileyWM.html
  World Wars I & II

Fimber

See Wetwang

Flockton

- War Memorials in the Wakefield Area: Flockton War Memorial
  freepages.history.rootsweb.com/~framland/flo.htm
  World War I. Also at:
  www.wdfhs.co.uk/flo.htm

Folkton

- Folkton Parish: Folkton - Flixton War Memorial Transcription
  www.genuki.org.uk/big/eng/YKS/ERY/Folkton/
  WMFolkton__FlixtonWM1.html
  World Wars I & II

Fryston

- War Memorials in the Wakefield Area: Fryston War Memorial,
  St. Peter's Church
  freepages.history.rootsweb.com/~framland/fry.htm
  World War I. Also at:
  www.wdfhs.co.uk/fry.htm

Gargrave

- Gargrave Parish: Gargrave War Memorial Transcription
  www.genuki.org.uk/big/eng/YKS/WRY/Gargrave/
  WMGargraveWM__0.html

  World Wars I & II

- Gargrave Parish: Gargrave Roll of Honour Transcriptions
  www.genuki.org.uk/big/eng/YKS/WRY/Gargrave/
  RoHGargraveStAndrewROH.html

  World War I

- Gargrave Parish: Gargrave Memorial Plaque Transcription
  www.genuki.org.uk/big/eng/YKS/WRY/Gargrave/
  MPGargraveStAndrewWMPlaque.html

  World War II

Gildersome

See Batley

Gisburn

- Gisburn Parish: Gisburn Roll of Honour Transcriptions
  www.genuki.org.uk/big/eng/YKS/WRY/Gisburn/
  RoHGisburnStMaryROH.html

  World War I

- Gisburn Parish: Gisburn War Memorial Transcriptions
  www.genuki.org.uk/big/eng/YKS/WRY/Gisburn/WMGisburnWM__0.html
  World Wars I & II

Great Ayton

- Greatayton Parish: Greatayton Memorial Plaque Transcription
  www.genuki.org.uk/big/eng/YKS/NRY/Greatayton/
  MPGreatAytonAllSaintsWMPlaque__2.html

Great Driffield

- Great Driffield Parish: Great Driffield War Memorial Transcription
  www.genuki.org.uk/big/eng/YKS/ERY/Greatdriffield/WMDriffieldWM1.html
  World War I

Great Hatfield

- Sigglesthorne Parish: Great Hatfield War Memorial Transcription
  www.genuki.org.uk/big/eng/YKS/ERY/Sigglesthorne/
  WMGreatHatfieldWM.html
  World War I

Greetland

- Greetland War Memorial
  www.hamm25.freeserve.co.uk/greetland__war__memorial1.htm

Grimethorpe

- War Memorials in the Wakefield Area: Grimethorpe War Memorial
  freepages.history.rootsweb.com/~framland/gri.htm
  World Wars I & II. Also at:
  www.wdfhs.co.uk/gri.htm

Gristhorpe

- Filey Parish: Gristhorpe War Memorial Transcription
  www.genuki.org.uk/big/eng/YKS/NRY/FileyWMGristhorpeWM1.html
  World Wars I & II

Guisborough

- [Guisborough]: War Memorials Search Results Page
  www.war-memorials.org.uk/
  Click on 'Cleveland' and 'Guisborough'

Hackness

- Hackness Parish: Hackness Memorial Plaque Transcription
  www.genuki.org.uk/big/eng/YKS/NRY/Hackness/
  MPHacknessPlaque.html
  World War I

- Hackness Parish: Hackness War Memorial Transcription
  www.genuki.org.uk/big/eng/YKS/NRY/Hackness/WMHacknessWM1.html
  World War I

Halton West

- Long Preston Parish: Halton West War Memorial Transcriptions
  www.genuki.org.uk/big/eng/YKS/WRY/Longpreston/
  WMHaltonWestChapelUnknownPlusWM.html

Harpham

- Harpham Parish: Harpham Memorial Plaque Transcription
  www.genuki.org.uk/big/eng/YKS/ERY/Harpham/MPHarphamWM.html
  World War I

Harrogate

- Knaresborough Parish: Harrogate Memorial Plaque Transcriptions
  www.genuki.org.uk/big/eng/YKS/WRY/Knaresborough/
  MPHarrogateStPeterWMPlaque__0.html

- Knaresborough Parish: Harrogate Memorial Plaque Transcriptions
  www.genuki.org.uk/big/eng/YKS/WRY/Knaresborough/
  MPHarrogateStPeterWMPlaqueRN.html
  Royal Naval Association plaque

- Knaresborough Parish: Harrogate War Memorial Transcriptions
  www.genuki.org.uk/big/eng/YKS/WRY/Knaresborough/
  WMHarrogateWM__0.html
  World Wars I & II

- St. Peter's Harrogate: Memorials for Ever to "The Glorious Dead" of the Great War
  www.genuki.org.uk/big/eng/YKS/Misc/Transcriptions/WRY/
  HarrogateStPeterWMInfo.html

- Knaresborough Parish: Harrogate War Memorial Transcriptions
  www.genuki.org.uk/big/eng/YKS/WRY/Knaresborough/
  WMHarrogateAshvilleCollegeWM__0.html
  World Wars I & II. Ashville College memorial

Havercroft

See Ryhill

Haworth

- Bradford Parish: Haworth Memorial Plaque Transcription
  www.genuki.org.uk/big/eng/YKS/WRY/Bradford/
  MPHaworthStMichaelWMPlaque__2.html
  World Wars I & II

- Bradford Parish: Haworth War Memorial Transcription
  www.genuki.org.uk/big/eng/YKS/WRY/Bradford/WMHaworthWM__0.html
  World War I

- Bradford Parish: Haworth Roll of Honour Transcription
  www.genuki.org.uk/big/eng/YKS/WRY/Bradford/
                              RoHHaworthStMichaelROH.html
  World Wars I & II

Haxby
- To the Glory of God and in Grateful Remembrance of these men of the
  Parish of Haxby who laid down their lives in the Great War A.D.
  1914-1919
  www.haxby-york.co.uk/religion/ww1memorialindex.html

Hebden
- Linton in Coaven Parish: Hebden Memorial Plaque Transcription
  www.genuki.org.uk/big/eng/YKS/WRY/Lintonincraven/
                              MPHebdenStPeterWMPlaque.html

Hellifield
- Long Preston Parish: Hellifield War Memorial Transcription
  www.genuki.org.uk/big/eng/YKS/WRY/Longpreston/
                              WMHellifieldWM__0.html

  World War II

Hemsworth
- Hemsworth War Memorial
  www.wdfhs.co.uk/hem.htm

High Bentham
  See Low Bentham

Hollym
- Hollym Parish: Hollym Memorial Plaque Transcription
  www.genuki.org.uk/big/eng/YKS/ERY/Hollym/MPHollymRoH.html

Horbury
- War Memorials in the Wakefield Area: Horbury South African War
  Memorial
  freepages.history.rootsweb.com/~framland/horsa.htm

- Horbury War Memorial
  www.wdfhs.co.uk/hor.htm

Horbury Bridge
- War Memorials in the Wakefield Area: Horbury Bridge War Memorial
  freepages.history.rootsweb.com/~framland/horb.htm
  World War II. Also at:
  www.wdfhs.co.uk/horb.htm

Horton in Ribblesdale
- Horton in Ribblesdale Parish: Horton in Ribblesdale Memorial Plaque
  Transcriptions
  www.genuki.org.ui/big/eng/YKS/WRY/Hortoninribblesdale/
                              MPHortonInRibblesdaleMPlaque.html

  World War I

Hotham
- Hotham Parish: Hotham War Memorial Transcription
  www.genuki.org.uk/big/eng/YKS/ERY/Hotham/WMHothamWM1.html
  World Wars I & II

Howarth
- War Memorials in the Wakefield Area: Mount Zion Methodist Church
  War Memorial: Howarth's Chapel of Rest
  freepages.history.rootsweb.com/~framland/zion.htm
  World Wars I & II. Also at:
  www.wdfhs.co.uk/zion.htm

Howden
- Howden Parish: Howden War Memorial Transcription
  www.genuki.org.uk/big/eng/YKS/ERY/Howden/
                              WMWMHowden2CarolineHaywood.html

  World Wars I & II

Hubberholme
  See Arncliffe

Hunmanby

- Hunmanby War Memorial
  www.hunmanby.com/memorial.html
  World Wars I & II

- Hunmanby Parish: Hunmanby War Memorial Transcription
  www.genuki.org.uk/big/eng/YKS/ERY/Hunmanby/WMHunmanbyWM.html

Kilham

- Kilham Parish: Kilham War Memorial Transcription
  www.genuki.org.uk/big/eng/YKS/ERY/Kilham/MPKilhamRoH14-18.html
  World War I

Kinsley

- War Memorials in the Wakefield Area: Kinsley War Memorial
  freepages.history.rootsweb.com/~framland/kin.htm
  World Wars I & II. Also at:
  www.wdfhs.co.uk/kin.htm

Kirby Grindalythe

- Kirby Grindalythe Parish: Kirby Grindalythe Memorial Plaque
  Transcription
  www.genuki.org.uk/big/eng/YKS/ERY/Kirbygrindalythe/
  MPKirbyGrindalytheWM.html
  World Wars I & II

Kirby Misperton

- Kirby Misperton Parish: Kirby Misperton Memorial Plaque
  Transcription
  www.genuki.org.uk/big/eng/YKS/NRY/Kirbymisperton/
  MPKirbyMispertonWM.html
  World War I

Kirkhamgate

War Memorials in the Wakefield Area: Kirkhamgate War Memorial
freepages.history.rootsweb.com/~framland/kirk.htm
World War I. Also at:
www.wdfhs.co.uk/kirk.htm

Knaresborough

- Knaresborough Online Roll of Honour
  www.knaresborough.co.uk/history/rollofhonour/
  World Wars I & II

- Knaresborough Cenotaph
  gye.future.easyspace.com/KnCen.htm
  World Wars I & II

- Knaresborough Parish: Knaresborough Memorial Plaque Transcription
  www.genuki.org.uk/big/eng/YKS/WRY/Knaresborough/
  MPHarrogateStPaulsWestrdURCWMPlaque__1.html
  World Wars I & II

Knottingley

- War Memorials in the Wakefield Area: Knottingley War Memorial
  freepages.history.rootsweb.com/~framland/kno.htm
  World Wars I & II. Also at
  www.wdfhs.co.uk/kno.htm

- War Memorials in the Wakefield Area: Knottingley St. Botolphs Church
  War Memorials
  freepages.history.rootsweb.com/~framland/stbot.htm
  World War I. Also at:
  www.wdfhs.co.uk/stbot.htm

Langtoft

- Langtoft Parish: Langtoft War Memorial Transcription
  www.genuki.org.uk/big/eng/YKS/ERY/Langtoft/WMLangtoftWM1.html
  world Wars I & II

- Langtoft Parish: Langtoft Memorial Plaque Transcription
  www.genuki.org.uk/big/eng/YKS/ERY/Langtoft/MPLangtoftRoH.html

Lastingham

See Appleton le Moors

Leven

- Leven War Memorial
  www.leven-village.co.uk/village/churches/memorial.htm
  World Wars I & II

- Leven Parish: Leven War Memorial Transcription
  www.genuki.org.uk/big/eng/YKS/ERY/Leven/WMLevenWM1.html

Low Bentham
- Low Bentham Parish: High Bentham Memorial Plaque Transcription
  www.genuki.org.uk/big/eng/YKS/WRY/Lowbentham/
                    MPHighBenthamStMargaretWMPlaque.html
  World War I

Low Catton
- Low Catton Parish: Low Catton War Memorial
  www.genuki.org.uk/big/eng/YKS/ERY/Lowcatton/WMCattonsWM.html
  World War I

Luddenden
- Luddenden & Midgley War Memorial
  www.hamm25.freeserve.co.uk/Luddmem.htm

Luddenden Foot
- Luddendenfoot War Memorial
  www.hamm25.freeserve.co.uk/LFoot.htm

Mappleton
- Mappleton Parish: Mappleton Memorial Plaque
  www.genuki.org.uk/big/eng/YKS/ERY/Mappleton/
                    MPMappletonallSaintsRoH.html
  World War I

Marton
- Sinnington Parish: Marton Memorial Plaque Transcription
  www.genuki.org.uk/big/eng/YKS/NRY/Sinnington/
                    MPMartonMissionWM.html
  World War I

Methley
- War Memorials in the Wakefield Area: Methley War Memorial
  freepages.history.rootsweb.com/~framland/met.htm
  World War I. Also at:
  www.wdfhs.co.uk/met.htm

Midgley
  See Luddenden

Moorthorpe
  See South Emsall

Muston
- Muston Parish: Muston War Memorial Transcription
  www.genuki.org.uk/big/eng/YKS/ERY/Muston/WMMustonWM.html
  World War I

Newmillardam
- War Memorials in the Wakefield Area: Newmillardam War Memorial
  freepages.history.rootsweb.com/~framland/new.htm
  World Wars I & II. Also at:
  www.wdfhs.co.uk/new.htm

Norland
- Norland War Memorial
  www.hamm25.freeserve.co.uk/norland.htm

Normanton
- War Memorials in the Wakefield Area: Normanton War Memorial
  freepages.history.rootsweb.com/~framland/nor.htm
  World Wars I & II. Also at:
  www.wdfhs.co.uk/nor.htm

North Elmsall
- War Memorials in the Wakefield Area: North Elmsall Memorial
  freepages.history.rootsweb.com/~framland/newm.htm
  World War I. Also at:
  www.wdfhs.co.uk/newm.htm

North Ferriby
- North Ferriby Parish: North Ferriby War Memorial Transcription
  www.genuki.org.uk/big/eng/YKS/ERY/Northferriby/
                    WMNorthFerribyWM__bothwars__1.html
  World Wars I & II

Northallerton
- Northerallerton Parish: Northallerton War Memorial Transcription
  www.genuki.org.uk/big/eng/YKS/NRY/Northallerton/
                    WMNorthallertonRoH1.html
  World Wars I & II

- Northallerton Memorials Project
  www.scmetcalfe.btinternet.co.uk/
  War Memorials

Nunkeeling
- Nunkeeling Parish: Bewholme War Memorial Transcription
www.genuki.org.uk/big/eng/YKS/ERY/Nunkeeling/WMBewholmeWM.html
World War I

Old Ellerby
- Swine Parish: Old Ellerby Memorial Plaque Transcription
www.genuki.org.uki/big.eng/YKS/ERY/Swine/WMOldEllerbyWM1.html
World War I

Ormesby
- [St. Cuthberts Parish Chruch, Ormesby:] War Memorials Search Results
Page
www.war-memorials.org.uk/
click on 'Teesside' and place

Ossett
- War Memorials in the Wakefield Area: Ossett War Memorial
freepages.history.rootsweb.com/~framland/oss.htm
World Wars I & II. Also at:
www.wdfhs.co.uk/oss.htm

Outwood
- War Memorials in the Wakefield Area: Memorial in the Church of
St. Mary Magdalene, Outwood
freepages.history.rootsweb.com/~framland/osmm.htm
World Wars I & II

- War Memorials in the Wakefield Area: Outwood Methodist Church War
Memorial
freepages.history.rootsweb.com/~framland/fit.htm
World War I. Also at:
freepages.history.rootsweb.com/~framland/outmeth.htm
And at:
www.wdfhs.co.uk/outmeth.htm

Patrington
- Patrington Parish: Patrington Memorial Plaque transcription
www.genuki.org.uk/big/eng/YKS/ERY/Patrington/
MPPatringtonRoH14-18.html
World Wars I & II

Pontefract
- War Memorials in the Wakefield Area: Memorial in All Saints Church,
Pontefract
freepages.history.rootsweb.com/~framland/ponas.htm
World Wars I & II

Pudsey
- Calverley Parish: Pudsey War Memorial Transcription
www.genuki.org.uk/big/eng/YKS/WRY/Calverley/WMPudseyDummy.html
World Wars I & II

Rawcliffe
- Snaith Parish: Rawcliffe War Memorial Transcription
www.genuki.org.uk/big/eng/YKS/WRY/Snaith/WMRawcliffeWM3.html
World Wars I & II. Includes separate pages for many individuals
commemorated

Reighton
- Reighton Parish: Reighton War Memorial Transcription
www.genuki.org.uk/big/eng/YKS/ERY/Reighton/
WMReightonStPeterWM.html
World Wars I & II

Rillington
- Rillington Parish: Rillington Memorial Plaque Transcription
www.genuki.org.uk/big/eng/YKS/ERY/Rillington/MPRillingtonRoH.html
World War I

Rishworth
- Rishworth War Memorial
www.hamm25.freeserve.co.uk/Rishworth.htm

Romanby
- The Romanby War Memorial
www.scmetcalfe.btinternet.co.uk
Click on title

Rosedale

- Lastingham Parish: Rosedale Abbey War Memorial Transcription
  www.genuki.org.uk/big/eng/YKS/NRY/Lastingham/
                                           WMRosedaleWM__0.html
  World Wars I & II, and Korean War

Royston

- War Memorials in the Wakefield Area: Royston War Memorial
  freepages.history.rootsweb.com/~framland/roy.htm
  World War I & II. Also at:
  www.wdfhs.co.uk/roy.htm

Rudston

- Rudston Parish: Rudston War Memorial Transcription
  www.genuki.org.uk/big/eng/YKS/ERY/Rudston/WMRudstonWM.html

Ryhill

- War Memorials in the Wakefield Area: Ryhill and Havercroft War
  Memorial
  freepages.history.rootsweb.com/~framland/ryh.htm
  World War I. Also at:
  www.wdfhs.co.uk/ryh.htm

Sandal Magna

- War Memorials in the Wakefield Area: War Memorial inside St. Helen's
  Church, Sandal, Wakefield
  freepages.history.rootsweb.com/~framland/wakstj.htm
  World Wars I & II. Also at:
  www.wdfhs.co.uk/wakstj.htm

- War Memorials in the Wakefield Area: Sandal Wesleyan Church Organ
  freepages.history.rootsweb.com/~framland/sanwes.htm
  World War I memorial. Also at:
  www.wdfhs.co.uk/sanwes.htm

Scampston

- Rillington Parish: Scampston Memorial Plaque Transcription
  www.genuki.org.uk/big/eng/YKS/ERY/Rillington/MPScampstonRoH1.html
  World Wars I & II

Scarborough

- Scarborough Parish: Scarborough War Memorial Transcription
  www.genuki.org.uk/big/eng/YKS/NRY/Scarborough/
                                           WMScarboroughOliversMountWM1.html
  World Wars I & II

Scawton

- Scawton Parish: Scawton War Memorial Transcription
  www.genuki.org.uk/big/eng/YKS/NRY/Scawton/WMScawtonWM.html
  World War I

Sewerby

- Bridlington Parish: Sewerby War Memorial Transcription
  www.genuki.org.uk/big/eng/YKS/ERY/Bridlington/WMSewerbyWM.html
  World Wars I & II

Sharlston

- War Memorials in the Wakefield Area: Sharlston War Memorial
  freepages.history.rootsweb.com/~framland/sha.htm
  World Wars I & II. Also at:
  www.wdfhs.co.uk/sha.htm

Shepley

- Kirkburton Parish: Shepley War Memorial Transcription
  www.genuki.org.uk/big/eng/YKS/WRY/Kirkburton/WMShepley3RW.html
  World Wars I & II

Sigglesthorne

- Sigglesthorne Parish: Sigglesthorne War Memorial Transcription
  www.genuki.org.uk/big/eng/YKS/ERY/Sigglesthorne/
                                           WMSigglesthorneWM.html
  World War I

Skidby

- Skidby Parish; Skidby War Memorial Transcription
  www.genuki.org.uk/big/eng/YKS/ERY/Skidby/WMSkidby/WM1.html
  World Wars I & II

Skirlaugh
  See Swine

Sledmere
- Sledmere Parish: Sledmere Roll of Honour Transcription
  www.genuki.org.uk/big/eng/YKS/ERY/Sledmere/RoHSledmereRoH.html

Slingsby
- Slingsby Parish: Slingsby Memorial Plaque Transcription
  www.genuki.org.uk/big/eng/YKS/NRY/Slingsby/
  MPSlingsbyAllSaintsRoH.html
  World War I

Snydale
See Streethouse

South Emsall
- War Memorials in the Wakefield Area: South Emsall & Moorthorpe
  War Memorial
  freepages.history.rootsweb.com/~framland/sem.html
  World Wars I & II. Also at:
  www.wdfhs.co.uk/sem.html

South Hiendley
- War Memorials in the Wakefield Area: South Hiendley War Memorial
  freepages.history.rootsweb.com/~framland/shei.htm
  World Wars I & II. Also at:
  www.wdfhs.co.uk/shei.htm

South Kirby
- South Kirby & Moorthorpe War Memorial
  www.wdfhs.co.uk/skm.htm

South Milford
- South Milford Soldiers & Sailors: Roll of Honour 1914-1918
  www.southmilford.co.uk/
  Click on 'History' and title

South Ossett
- War Memorials in the Wakefield Area: South Ossett War Memorial
  freepages.history.rootsweb.com/~framland/southoss.htm
  World War I

- War Memorials in the Wakefield Area: St. John's Methodist Church,
  South Ossett War Memorial
  freepages.history.rootsweb.com/~framland/ossmeth.htm
  World Wars I & II

Speeton
- Bridlington Parish: Speeton Roll of Honour Transciption
  www.genuki.org.uk/big/eng/YKS/ERY/Bridlington/ROHSpeetonRoH2.html
  World Wars I & II

Sproatley
- Sproatley Parish: Sproatley War Memorial Transcription
  www.genuki.org.uk/big/eng/YKS/ERY/Sproatley/WMSproatleyWM2.html
  World War I

Stanley
- War Memorials in the Wakefield Area: Stanley War Memorial
  freepages.history.rootsweb.com/~framland/stan.htm
  World War I. Also at:
  www.wdfhs.co.uk/stan.htm

- St. Peter's Church, Starley, War Memorial
  www.wdfhs.co.uk/stanley.htm
  World War I and II

Stillingfleet
- Stillingfleet Parish: Stillingfleet War Memorial Transcription
  www.genuki.org.uk/big/eng/YKS/ARY/Stillinglfeet/
  WMAcasterSelbyWM.html
  World War I

Streethouse
- War Memorials in the Wakefield Area: Streethouse & Snydale War
  Memorial
  freepages.history.rootsweb.com/~framland/str.htm
  World Wars I & II. Also at:
  www.wdfhs.co.uk/str.htm

Swine
- Swine Parish: Skirlaugh War Memorial Transcription
  www.genuki.org.uk/big/eng/YKS/ERY/Swine/WMSkirlaughWM1.html
  World Wars I & II

Swinefleet
- Whitgift Parish: Swinefleet War Memorial Transcription
www.genuki.org.uk/big/eng/YKS/WRY/Whitgift/
WMSwinefleet2CarolineHaywood1989.html
World Wars I & II

Thornes
- War Memorials and Cenotaphs in the Wakefield area: St James' Church
War Memorial
www.wdfhs.co.uk/thor.htm

Thorpe Bassett
- Thorpe Bassett Parish: Thorpe Bassett Memorial Plaque Transcription
www.genuki.org.uk/big/eng/YKS/ERY/ThorpebassettWM.html
World War I

Ulleskelf
- Ulleskelf Parish: Ulleskelf War Memorial Transcription
www.genuki.org.uk/big/eng/YKS/WRY/Ulleskelf/WMUlleskelfWM.html
World War I

Wakefield
- Central Wakefield War Memorial
www.wdfhs.co.uk/wak.htm

- Memorial in Manygates School, Wakefield
www.wdfhs.co.uk/man.htm

- War Memorials in the Wakefield Area: St. Catherines Church War
Memorial, Belle Vue, Wakefield
freepages.history.rootsweb.com/~framland/bell.htm
World War I. Also at:
www.wdfhs.co.uk/bell.htm

- War Memorials in the Wakefield Area: Thornes House School Roll of
Honour (now) Wakefield College, Thornes Park Centre
freepages.historyrootsweb.com/~framland/thsch.htm
World War I. Also at:
www.wdfhs.co.uk/thsch.htm

- War Memorials in the Wakefield Area: Queen Elizabeth Grammar
School War Memorial
freepages.history.rootsweb.com/~framland/que.htm
World Wars I & II. Also at:
www.wdfhs.co.uk/que.htm

- War Memorials in the Wakefield Area: St. Austin's Church War
Memorial, Wentworth Terrace
freepages.history.rootsweb.com/~framland/aus.htm
World War I. Also at:
www.wdfhs.co.uk/aus.htm

Walkington
- Walkington Parish: Walkington War Memorial Transcription
www.genuki.org.uk/big/eng/YKS/ERY/Walkington/
WMWalkingtonWM3.html
World Wars I & II, and Korean War

Walton
- War Memorials in the Wakefield Area: Walton War Memorial
freepages.history.rootsweb.com/~framland/wal.htm
World Wars I & II. Also at:
www.wdfhs.co.uk/wal.htm

Warmfield cum Heath
- War Memorials in the Wakefield Area: Warmfield cum Heath War
Memorial
freepages.history.rootsweb.com/~framland/warm.htm
World Wars I & II. Also at:
www.wdfhs.co.uk/warm.htm

West Bretton
- War Memorials in the Wakefield Area: West Bretton War Memorial
freepages.history.rootsweb.com/~framland/bre.htm
World Wars I & II. Also at:
www.wdfhs.co.uk/bre.htm

Wetwang

- Wetwang Parish: Fimber Memorial Plaque Transcription
  www.genuki.org.yuk/big/eng/YKS/ERY/Wetwang/MPFimberWM1.html
  World War I

Whitwood

- War Memorials in the Wakefield Area: Whitwood War Memorial
  freepages.history.rootsweb.com/~framland/whi.htm
  Also at:
  www.wdfhs.co.uk/whi.htm

Wooley

- War Memorials in the Wakefield Area: Wooley War Memorial
  freepages.history.rootsweb.com/~framland/wol.htm
  World Wars I & II. Also at:
  www.wdfhs.co.uk/wol.htm

Wragby

- War Memorials in the Wakefield Area: Wragby War Memorial
  freepages.history.rootsweb.com/~framland/wra.htm
  World Wars I & II. Also at:
  www.wdfhs.co.uk/wra.htm

- War Memorials in the Wakefield Area: Memorial in the Church of
  St. Michael and Our Lady, Wragby
  freepages.history.rootsweb.com/~framland/smolw.htm
  World War I. Transcript of roll of honour forthcoming

Wrenthorpe

- War Memorials in the Wakefield Area: St. Anne's Parish Church,
  War Memorial, Wrenthorpe
  freepages.history.rootsweb.com/~framland/stannes.htm
  World Wars I & II. Also at:
  www.wdfhs.co.uk/stannes.htm

- War Memorials in the Wakefield Area: Wrenthorpe St. Paul's Church
  War Memorials
  freepages.history.rootsweb.com/~framland/wrenwm.htm
  World Wars I & II.

- War Memorials in the Wakefield Area: Wrenthorpe Colliery War
  Memorial, St. John's Church, Wentworth Street/St. John's Square
  freepages.history.rootsweb.com/~framland/wre.htm
  World War I. Also at:
  www.wdfhs.co.uk/wre.htm